November 20

HEALING A DISCOURAGED HEART

GETTING BACK ON TRACK
WHEN LIFE LETS YOU DOWN

GLADYS FAMORIYO

From Monica with love

Arise and shine young Lady, for your light has come & the glory of The Lord is risen upon you.

First published in Great Britain in 2011
By GF Books Ltd – *Changing lives through words*
Newmarket 4,
Keys Business Village,
Keys Park Road,
Hednesford,
Staffordshire, WS12 2HA
United Kingdom
Tel: +44 (0)870 750 1969
www.gladysfbooks.com

1 3 5 7 9 10 8 6 4 2

© Gladys Famoriyo

All rights reserved. No part of this book may be transmitted or reproduced in any form by any means without permission in writing from the publisher

Printed and bound in Great Britain by MPG Biddles Ltd. King's Lynn

ISBN 978-0-9562606-3-5

Type design and layout: www.hereandnowdesign.com

Scripture quotations marked (NTL) are taken from the Holy Bible, New Living Translation, © 1996, 2004, 2007 by Tyndale House Foundation. Used by permission of Tyndale House Publishers, Inc., Carol Stream, Illinois 60188. All rights reserved.

Scripture quotations marked (NKJV™) are taken from the New King James Version®. Copyright © 1982 by Thomas Nelson, Inc. Used by permission. All rights reserved.

Scripture quotations marked (MSG) are taken from The Message, copyright © Eugene H. Peterson. Published by Nav Press, Colorado Springs, Colorado, in association with Alive Communications, Colorado Springs, Colorado. Permission sought.

Scripture quotations marked (AMP) are taken from the Amplified Bible, copyright © 1954, 1958, 1962, 1964, 1965, 1987 by The Lockman Foundation. Used by permission

Contents

Dedication 5
Acknowledgements 6
Preface 8
How to get the best out of this book 12
Introduction 16

Part 1: Understanding Discouragement
Chapter 1: The many faces of discouragement 24
Chapter 2: Understanding the phases of discouragement 40

Part 2: Preparing for your journey
Chapter 3: Spiritual truths about God 60
Chapter 4: Essential truths about Life 75

Part 3: Strategies to develop an encouraged heart
Chapter 5: Getting Back On Track 94
Chapter 6: Digging Deeper 105

Part 4: Strength for the journey
Chapter 7: Journeying into our tomorrows 146
Chapter 8: Nuggets to strengthen your heart 171
Chapter 9: Uplifting scriptures 191
Afterword 201

About the author 208
Also available from the author 210

Dedication

I am dedicating this book to my wonderful parents.

My late father, Pastor Jonathan Famoriyo, whom I miss so dearly. Time alone will tell the impact you made on me. By watching you encourage countless people worldwide, I too can continue in your footsteps, with that legacy you left behind, to touch the lives of many others. Your beacon continues to shine into the lives of many, years after your passing.

My mother, Pastor Joyce Famoriyo, continues to remain a tower of strength and a source of joy – the one constant in my ever-changing world. A pillar of unshakable faith. How do I repay you for your undying love, relentless support, and never-ending prayers? Thank you for constantly believing in me. You have been the giant whose shoulders I have been able to stand on, to do the things God has placed in my heart. Because you stand, I too can stand. Your best days lie ahead of you and I will be by your side celebrating the great things God has already started in your life.

Acknowledgements

Father God, where would I be if not for Your grace? Your faithfulness and loving kindness astounds me daily. Because of You, I am able to *run through troops and leap over walls*. Year in year out, You remain true to Your word – be it Your written word or the ones You whisper softly into my heart. Your Spirit has been the wind beneath my wings that has allowed me to soar when life happened! Thank You for always being by my side, working Your plan out for my life. Daily, You surprise me and I will forever be in awe of You. My heart sings You a love song.

Hearty thanks go out to my family: Mother dearest (Pastor Joyce); my brother Sam; and sisters, along with their spouses – Deborah and Wale, Elizabeth and Mike, and Sarah and Kola (not forgetting my nephews and niece). Thanks for your continued support through the years. To all my aunties, uncles and cousins, you have been a blessing.

To my knowledgeable and awesome friends who helped me with this book: Dola Akinnibosun and Theresa Henshaw. Your labours of love will forever remain in my heart. Thanks for being there, as always.

Wanda (the 'Manuscript Doctor' and a true wonder) – all I can say is 'wow'. You may not know this but you have been a blessing to me, an answered prayer. Your creativity and endless 'contacts' amaze me. Thank you for going over and above the call of duty. Sarah, thanks for the seeds you sowed in shaping this book when it was in its embryonic form. I know from that one manuscript, many will follow. Natasha, James and Amanda, thank you for your creativity in helping me put the book together in such awesome way.

A special thanks to Rev. Yemi Adedeji, Sharon Platt-McDonald and Rev. Celia Apeagyei-Collins for your unyielding support, sound advice and relentless prayers. Lastly, to everyone else who has contributed in one way or another on this journey, including (but not limited to) my pastors, mentors, and coaches, I say thank you.

Preface

I wrote this book as a follow-up to *Overcoming Emotional Baggage: A Woman's Guide To Living The Abundant Life* when I realised that, for Christians especially, some of our emotional turmoil is caused by a disparity between our spiritual beliefs and hopes and the reality of our problems here on Earth. We hope and pray with all our might and although we do win some battles, there are others we lose or simply feel are never-ending.

When you're struggling with everyday challenges and seemingly unanswered prayers, you may start to wonder where God is in all of this. Why does He choose to remain silent at times? Why doesn't He do something like send a multitude of angels to our rescue? (Well, actually, just one would be nice – after all, He has done it in the past.)

Life becomes harder when, as a Christian, you experience a crisis of faith. At such times, questions such as: 'Why have You abandoned me?'; 'Do You really care?'; 'Can I trust You?'; or 'Are You real?' may start to drift through your mind. When a life crisis strikes and you look upwards for some sort of sign or answer, you may also be drawn to look inwards, searching for an indication that it has arisen because of something you've done, some sin or disobedience perhaps. Whether you do it consciously or not, you can find yourself thinking that you have brought the problem on yourself, that it is all your fault.

Over time, we realise that, as well as having to struggle with everyday challenges and seemingly unanswered prayers, many of our struggles are a manifestation of those deep-seated hurts or childhood memories that lie buried deep on the inside – many of which never see the light of day and are never voiced. Nevertheless, it is only a matter of time before they show themselves through our attitudes, beliefs and behaviours. And with all of this going on in our lives, it is no surprise that we see the seeds of discouragement take root deep within our hearts.

Maybe you have been faced with disappointment. Maybe you have watched a cherished dream or relationship slip away from you. Maybe you have a longstanding and/or pressing need. Maybe you are worn out from your struggles and no longer have the will or desire to carry on. Or like Asaph, you started to question the point of 'keeping your heart pure' when all you seem to get is trouble in return *(Psalm 73:13–14)* – and others around you seem to have no problems whatsoever.

If this where you are today, I want to start off by sharing some simple truths:

•	God is still God regardless of your personal experiences. His abilities have not diminished through time

•	God never abandons His own (though you may feel abandoned at times). He remains faithful

•	God hears every one of your cries – both audible and inaudible

•	God cares! He has always been concerned about you and will continue to be so

•	God can heal your discouraged heart and troubled soul.

The fact is, life can hurt at times and our experiences may discourage us. This being so, it makes sense to learn simple truths and strategies we can use on our journey through life, to not only safeguard us from discouragement but restore our hearts too. And that is what this book is all about. As you read, my prayers are that you move beyond discouragement as you dig deep into the well of your heart. I pray that through this restorative experience, your heart will spring to life, be filled with joy and above all, smile again.

How to get the best out of this book

'... let God transform you into a new person by changing the way you think. Then you will learn to know God's will for you, which is good and pleasing and perfect.'
(*Romans 12:2, NLT*)

The first part of the book aims to shed light on discouragement: what it looks like and how it affects us. The second part of the book prepares you for the journey by providing you with some simple yet pertinent truths. The third part focuses on equipping you with practical truths and strategies to get you back on track.

To help you in your development, I have incorporated special 'moments' for you to reflect, learn and pray. The 'journaling moments' give you time to pause and listen to what your heart is saying; the 'enlightening moments' will give you some food for thought; and the 'praying moments' give you the opportunity to say a short prayer.

It is worth bearing in mind that the intention of this book is not to make your difficult life experiences, challenges and situations disappear. Rather, it is about considering certain notions and attitudes that will support you and help you navigate your way through them, so that these experiences do not rob you of your joy, peace and hope.

I encourage you to allow this book to transform you into a new person by changing the way you think. I pray that you become strengthened from the inside out, so that you can withstand the fiery darts life throws at you. Because the fact is, they will come. But with Gods help and strength, you can pass through them all and remain standing.

Praying moments

As we embark this journey, why not say this short prayer:

Dear Father,
I ask that You travel this journey with me. I pray that You heal my heart of the pain caused by … [insert your own list] … of my yesteryears, yesterdays and todays.

Let me feel Your presence as I take each step of the way. I grant you access to the recesses of my heart and soul. Please touch my heart and make it smile again. I ask that You help me get back on track so that I can experience true joy and peace even when the storms of life rage around me. I ask for strength and patient endurance so that I can stand the test of time. Finally, equip me for all that lies ahead in this journey called 'life' and help me face it confidently, knowing fully that You are with me, each step of the way.
Thank You, in advance, for answering my prayers.
In Jesus' precious name.
Amen.

Introduction

The fact is life can disappoint us. People leave, overlook, betray, reject or wrong us. Dreams and desires can fail to materialise. Battles are fought with no sign of an end in sight. Daily struggles can feel like an unrelenting battering ram on our souls which can knock us down. Though each time we rise again, the effect of each blow can persist until, over time, it can surface as discouragement.

If you have ever felt let down by life, love, people or even God, the chances are that you have experienced a discouraged heart. For you, like many others, the notion of discouragement is not a new one. It has been an age-old struggle for people from as far back as biblical times. David, who had his fair share of discouraging situations brought on by family, friend and foe, is a good example to take. You only need to glance through some of his Psalms to catch a glimpse of how depressed he got at times. And let's not forget the woes of Job or the anguishing cries of the prophet Jeremiah who was nicknamed the Weeping Prophet.

Discouragement seems to affect people from all walks of life: from the pulpit to the pews; both new and old believers; men and women; young and old. And if discouragement has been your experience, there is a chance you have joined many others bombarding Heaven with questions like:

'Why me?'
'Why now?'
'What's going on?'
'Where are You Lord?'
'Do You care?'

As I write this chapter, the plight of two women in two different situations come to mind. I believe they portray our challenges with life disappointments very well.

The first was a story from a movie called *Last Holiday*, featuring Queen Latifah as a retail assistant with big dreams. One day, she hit her head in a minor accident at work and was taken to hospital to rule out any major injuries. Unfortunately, after having a brain scan, she was given the wrong diagnosis and was told she only had a short time to live. Although this was only a movie, I felt her reaction was very typical, not just for Christians but for human beings in general. In church, her 'Why me?' and 'Why now?' questions surfaced. After all, as far as she was concerned she had been a 'good' Christian living a 'clean' life. She could not fathom why this was happening to her at this stage in her life, in her early thirties, when she was yet to fulfil her dreams, get married and so on.

Like the character in this movie, we don't get a news flash, email or text message warning us of what lies ahead (unless God chooses to reveal it to us). Life just happens and we have to deal with it – as unprepared as we are.

The second story was recounted in a book I read once. A Christian lady, who had been struggling with infertility for many years finally got pregnant. However, her joy was soon turned to grief when she was told at ten weeks that she had lost the baby. The word 'discouraged' couldn't possibly describe how she was feeling. This story came to mind when, just this week, I was told of a couple who had lost two babies, one of them in utero, in less than a year. Both of these unfortunate couples have had to start the painful journey of dealing with their loss. And, for the women, their difficult feelings or misgivings about their ability to give birth again will no doubt surface.

Over the years, I have watched people struggle with harrowing situations, some of which result in a loss of some kind (their health or loved one for instance).

I remember two separate occasions when a number of us were praying for a person to be healed from a serious medical condition. In both instances, the individuals died despite the fact that they had both made a significant recovery – they had actually gone back to living their 'normal' lives before suffering a relapse and dying shortly after. Those of us left behind were stunned, to say the least. Another opportunity for discouragement to creep in and take hold.

I know of people I hoped and prayed they would be healed before medical intervention (e.g. surgery) was required. But in the end, the surgery had to be carried out and they had to live the rest of their lives with the drastic outcome.

Many, including myself, have experienced longstanding personal struggles and unmet desires. If some of us were to be honest, I am sure we would admit to the fact that, as discouragement slips into our hearts from time to time, our strength and faith starts to wane over time.

Maybe you have your own life story (or two) to tell? It could be that you have bombarded Heaven with questions of your own. Maybe the impact of your personal experiences has left you exhausted, anxious, hopeless and stuck. It could be you are just going through the motions, carrying along with you a discouraged heart and troubled soul.

If this is the case I want to let you know that, despite it all, you can get over your discouraged heart. Wherever you find yourself today you can get back on track. With God, all things are indeed possible. Nothing is too hard for Him (*Jeremiah 32:27*). The Bible serves as a constant reminder of the fact that God can heal your discouraged heart (*Jeremiah 31:25*). I simply ask that you allow Him in to do one of the things He does best: mend hearts. In order for this to happen you have to grant Him access as the handle to the door of your heart is on the inside and only you can open it. This was the reason for saying the prayer earlier on.

However, before we dive into the 'how to' section of the book, I want to lay the foundation by helping you gain clarity on what discouragement looks like. So please keep your heart open.

PART 1

UNDERSTANDING DISCOURAGEMENT

Chapter 1

The many faces of discouragement

> 'Laughter can conceal a heavy heart:
> when the laughter ends, the grief remains.'
> *(Proverbs 14:13, NLT)*

One of the challenges some of us face is actually becoming aware of our discouraged hearts. For, when we lose sight of this we are not in a position to take the necessary action to move forward with our lives. To help us understand what discouragement looks like I want to give you a glimpse of what it looks like in the lives of four individuals, each of them facing different life challenges that have brought on discouragement.

'Did God really call me?'

Richard's story

Richard knew God had a special assignment for him, for he was a gifted speaker and had always felt drawn to serving in fulltime ministry. So it was no surprise he landed in Bible college. And by the end of his studies, Richard was ready to preach the Gospel.

But that was 13 years ago. Although he had been faithfully serving his pastor in his local church in team leadership roles, he felt his dream of pastoring a church ebbing away. Each of the many times he tried to raise the matter with his pastor he felt fobbed off with statements like: 'you are not ready'; 'it's not the right time'; or 'we need you here'. In recent years, Richard had started to resent his pastor for this, though he kept up his church attendance along with his leadership responsibilities. In actual fact, the passion Richard once had had gradually ebbed away, to be replaced with anger and disappointment towards God. It seemed that he had been forgotten. Deep within himself, he had also started to question whether he was called to the ministry.

Whilst Richard did a good job in concealing his feelings, behind closed doors the cracks were beginning to appear. He had lost his drive to read his Bible or pray. Nowadays, he took comfort in an old habit of his — drinking.

What is going on

Because of their deferred hopes and dreams, the 'Richards' of this world become eaten up with anger and bitter disappointment. At the same time, they become upset with those they pinned their hopes on, whether it be God or others. In Richards's case, he expected his pastor to ordain him and release him to start his ministry or, at the very least, to allow him to preach every now and again. Instead, Richard felt his pastor was only serving his own interests. Plus, it felt like God had chosen to take a backseat on the matter.

Like Richard, when we get weary and frustrated we find ourselves plunging into the valley of despair and discouragement. Many of us conceal this with our various masking techniques whilst trying to keep up a pretence. The sad thing is, of course, that the situation continues to eat us up deep inside.

Journaling moments

Have there been times when you have hoped for a dream or goal to come to fruition? Maybe you have held on to a promise of God's that you are still waiting to be fulfilled? If so, ponder on your own experiences. How has the experience affected you? What have been your own responses to the situation?

 Enlightening moments

When it comes to God, delay is not denial.

'I can't trust You.'

Lola's Story

Lola can be described as a self-made business mogul. At 45, she owns a string of successful businesses, has been featured on the cover of magazines, and has won several awards, including recently an OBE (Order of the British Empire) for her contributions to the business world and charitable projects.

Simply put, Lola has achieved an enviable amount of success in many areas – but with one exception: her love life. Lola had never dreamed she would be single, let alone childless, at her age. However, with a string of failed relationships that seem to fizzle out shortly after they started, she had begun to feel discouraged. The most recent had really broken her heart because it had seemed to her that Steve was all she had ever prayed for. Within no time, they had been making future plans together but then it had all gone wrong: Steve had gone cold on her and hadn't returned her calls. When she had finally tracked him down, all he had to say for the weeks of silence was that he had been busy. After that, she never heard from him again. Just like the others.

After the Steve episode and endless tears, Lola decided to give up on the whole marriage issue. As she really had believed that Steve was 'the one' she now felt she could no longer trust God on the matter. The thought of going through another heartbreak did not appeal to her. Instead, she decided to put all her focus on her businesses and charity work. However, with this decision she faced a whole new challenge: dealing with the well-meaning folk in her life who weren't about to give up. She certainly did not need another lecture from mother dearest on how God can and will do it. Nor did she need her pastor, or anyone else for that matter, telling her to keep on praying. In fact, it was going to take the grace of God for her not to tell them exactly what she thought on the matter!

What is going on

For Lola, the disparity between what she hoped for and the reality of the situation has led to a crisis of faith. Can she still trust God on the matter? Will He do it? Can He bring it to pass? These were the thoughts that floated about in her mind. Many 'Lolas' of this world come to the conclusion that God can't or won't. And so they convince themselves they can live without 'it' (whatever 'it' represents in their world: husband, healing, money, for example). Of course, these decisions are born out of disappointment – their discouraged hearts simply got tired of waiting for God to act.

A common pattern seems to be that they stop praying about the situation that's presenting the problem, although they will continue to pray and hope for changes in other aspects of their lives. Now to an observer, this might seem like they have decided to leave the matter firmly in God's hands, but that isn't actually the case. Instead their discouragement acts like a wall of resistance so that when God tries to reassure them that He will fulfil His promises to them, their hearts respond with, 'Whatever, God!', as opposed to responding the way Mary did in *Luke 1:38* where she said:

> 'I am the Lord's servant. May everything you have said about me come true.' (NLT)

To them, God simply becomes a promise-breaker –

One who simply can't be trusted.

 Journaling moments

Like Lola, have you given up on something you hoped for, justifying why you have done so in some way, and afterwards focused your attention on other things? Seeing that God sees and knows all things, isn't it time to become transparent before God? To get you started in this, first make a list of those things you feel you have actively or passively put aside, for whatever reason. Then I suggest you bring them before God. Find out what He wants you to do (for example: hope again; deal with your fears concerning the situation; or leave your request on the altar).

'When will it be my turn?'

Rachael's story

'Oh God,' Rachael thought. 'This can't be happening again! What about the prophetic word given to me, all the prayers, fasting and anointing of oil?' Rachael sobbed as she sank to the bathroom floor. Her fourth fertility treatment had failed again. All that money spent, the treatments, the hoping, yet fifteen years of marriage to Daniel and no child to show for it.

'Is my womb cursed? Have I sinned? Am I a bad person? Have I done something wrong? My sisters have all had children – why can't I?" These thoughts plagued Rachael's mind, day in, day out.

To make matters worse, lately, she and Daniel had been under tremendous pressure from his side of the family. According to her mother-in-law, it was shameful not to have children. When Rachael hadn't displayed a 'bump' in their first year of marriage, tongues had started to wag. As Daniel was the first born in his family, cultural tradition said that he should produce a male heir to keep the family name going. The last time his mother visited, Rachael overheard her suggesting to Daniel that he should marry another wife – a fertile girl from their village. After all, he was not the one with the problem – he already had a daughter before the couple met.

Whilst Daniel's Christian beliefs had dissuaded him from agreeing to his mother's suggestion, Rachael noticed a gradual change in his attitude towards her. She knew the 'child' issue was driving a wedge between them, hence she had been banking on the treatment working this time.

What is going on?

Today, many 'Rachael's' exist in the body of Christ. Whilst some battle with childlessness, others battle with other types of barrenness and fruitless efforts (unproductive results or unprofitable businesses, for instance). Whatever the case, they are confronted with their particular issue on a daily basis. It becomes a source of constant pressure, resulting in a nagging unrest deep within. Over time, they can become increasingly anxious and downcast though they may keep up the momentum of prayer, fasting, hoping and trusting.

The 'Rachaels' of our world also face another challenge: dealing with the consequences that arise from their issues. Like the woman with the issue of blood (*Luke 8: 42-48*) and Hannah (*1 Samuel 1*), they are sometimes subjected to humiliation, rejection, reproach, hostility, isolation, exclusion, ridicule and the insensitivity of others. To make matters worse, they are then pestered by a host of 'well-meaning' people suggesting they should try 'xyz' or up their game in the praying, fasting, believing, sowing, confessing, anointing, 'binding the devil', or deliverance department. It is no surprise when someone in just this sort of predicament starts to think that their situation has come about as a direct result of something lacking on their part. That, somehow, it is their fault. Then we start to see other symptoms show up such as guilt, self-doubt and confusion. And, alongside them, discouragement sets in. (Incidentally, while prayer and fasting are considered the norm for Christians, it is important that would-be 'encouragers' are more discerning when they speak.)

The last point I want to mention is there comes a time when, like the woman with the issue of blood, we can no longer rely on our 'works', efforts or actions to save us. It will take the awesome power of God to do so. So maybe, we just need to let go, let God in and let His peace guard our hearts as we trust Him to accomplish what might seem impossible.

Journaling moments

Reflective questions:

- can you picture living your life without the very thing you have been striving for or need God to do?

- could you keep serving God even if you don't get what you want, when you want it?

Tough questions but worth considering.

 Enlightening moments

God is not limited to 'yes' or 'no' answers nor black or white solutions – which our vision can be limited in seeing (a human trait). Rather, He works in many dimensions across a whole array of shades of grey, and even spectrums of colours we often fail to see. So maybe we need to let go and let Him be the ever-creative God we know Him to be.

'Why does waiting take so long?'

Jason's story

Jason stared gloomily at the latest rejection letter. After he had been laid off eighteen months ago, he always felt getting another job would be easy – after all, he was a competent engineer with over fifteen years industry experience. However, after attending interview after interview, his hope of finding a job and providing for his family seemed to be slipping away. And the thought of turning up at the job centre again to sign on was really taking its toll.

In the early days, Jason would fight back feelings of discouragement but today he was at an all time low. The scriptures he would normally quote to pep himself up didn't seem to be doing the trick. The fact was he was truly disappointed this time. He had prayed earnestly about this particular job and had been convinced that the job was his, especially after making it to the final round. The interview panel had actually told him, in so many words, that the job was his. What made the whole thing more upsetting was the fact that, although they said he was one of the best candidates they had seen, they had decided to give the job to an internal candidate. 'What a cheek!', he thought, to build his hopes up like that: showing him around, introducing him to staff, etc. That made it so much worse.

The job itself would have been perfect. With his new salary his family could have looked forward to buying another home as their last had been repossessed by the banks when they failed to make their mortgage repayments. The company car would have been a bonus too as they had had to sell their old one to make ends meet. Jason had planned to make this Christmas a special one for the family, with presents for the kids and new clothes for his wife, Lisa. But all those hopes had been dashed once again. He desperately wanted to 'be the man' and provide for his family, rather than receiving government benefits which barely met their needs. Before Jason knew it, he found himself retreating further into a 'cave', in an attempt to deal with his present reality.

What is going on?

Waiting on God can seem like a lifetime, especially when we need a quick response from above. And the longer we have to wait, the wearier we become. Jason had great intentions to provide for his family and try to restore some form of normality in their lives after losing his job, the family home and car – not to mention his confidence and self-esteem. He just never thought that eighteen months later he would still be jobless and a hundred per cent reliant on benefits.

The issue of waiting is a recurring theme for Christians and has been the culprit of many a discouraged heart. I remember once listening to a Christian song about waiting on God. I admit I initially scoffed at the thought: 'yeah right!' Now, before you crucify me, please understand where I was coming from. I had been waiting in line a long time to see my prayers and desires come to pass. I was tired and disappointed. And when I heard that song, I happened to be in a 'why-is-it-taking-so-long?' mode with God. But if I fast-forward a few years down the line, I most certainly see the value in waiting. I won't say I'm thrilled at the thought (God is still working on my patience!), but I would rather wait for God to perfect His work in me. (By the way, I am not saying this because I made it to the top of the line or got all that I wanted. I am still waiting!)

My encounter with the 'waiting' song and talking to people over the years have made me realise that most of us don't take well to the waiting game. While we may be happy to say we are 'waiting on the Lord' at the start of the journey, we start singing a different song after we have waited longer than we imagined we'd have to. Jason felt this way after waiting eighteen months for a job. He couldn't fathom what could be the reason for the holdup. But, the truth is that God always has a reason because He makes everything beautiful in its time (*Ecclesiastes 3:11*). The scripture goes on to say that He puts eternity in our hearts. Our challenge, as humans, is that we don't see the whole plan mapped out from start to finish.

Waiting, whilst maintaining our faith and standing strong till the very end, is our challenge. Jason began well, encouraging himself in the Lord, but like many of us, he did not expect to have to wait so long. The result was that his hands got weary and his knees got feeble. Later on, we will look at some principles, strategies and truths we can embrace to help us strengthen those amongst us with tired hands and encourage those amongst us with weak knees (*Isaiah 35:3*).

 ***Praying moments***

Allow the following scripture to comfort your heart.

'Yet I am confident I will see the Lord's goodness while I am here in the land of the living.'
(*Psalm 27: 13, NLT*)

As we come to the end of this chapter I am hoping that you start to see the different ways discouragement can surface in our lives as Christians. Bringing the focus back on you, now is a good time to pause and reflect on your own life. Have you experienced discouraging moments of your own? How has this affected you? Has it had an impact on the person we see today? Now is the time to connect (or reconnect) with your heart. Ask God to shine light on areas that have been hidden or are unknown to you.

Journaling moments

- can you relate to one or more of the different 'faces' of discouragement described above? If not, what has been your own personal experience with discouragement?

- describe how it affected you

- what lessons can you learn from both your experiences and what we have covered in this chapter?

Chapter 2

Understanding the phases of discouragement

'Hope deferred makes the heart sick
but a dream fulfilled is a tree of life.'
(Proverbs 13:12, NLT)

Building on the previous chapter, I want to use this one to highlight the feelings, thoughts and behaviours of discouraged individuals, based on my observations over the years. To simplify this, I have divided discouragement into three phases.

It helps to bear in mind that you may not experience all of the feelings, thought patterns, behaviours or even phases. Also, you may notice that some overlap which blurs the lines where one ends and another begins.

I believe our uniqueness as humans will determine how and what we encounter and the time spent in each phase. I feel several factors can contribute to this such as our faith and belief systems, personalities, life experiences, backgrounds, the support we have available and much more. And so, my suggestion is not to get hung up on ticking every box or getting into 'paralysis by analysis' but to use this as a simple signpost to understanding where you are at present, with a view of moving on.

The S.A.D. phase

This is the first phase we see when experiencing a discouraging situation. We may notice the onset immediately or over a period of time. The themes here are downheartedness, rationalising and dejection. I believe this phase is the normal human response to a distressing or tragic situation. In the Christendom, some carry the notion that we ought not to show any signs that we are being shaken or stirred by our experiences. This is always easy to say when the boot is on the other foot. Take, for example, Rachael (and the two couples I mentioned) who experienced the loss of their unborn child. It is natural to have a time to weep ... before one day being able to move on.

However, when we try to 'bottle up' our natural feelings and/or don't get the necessary support we need (from God and man), we may spend far too long in this phase, with some people struggling forever to get out. You hear people say they never got over their loss or grief. We need to make allowances for this and support each other to see the 'light at the end of the tunnel'.

Sadness

As its name suggests, this first part of the S.A.D. phase is characterised by unhappiness, hurt and pain, brought on by the situation we are facing or have faced. We see this occurring in the life of Rachael, whom we talked about earlier, who was distraught over the failure of her latest IVF treatment and the repercussions it had on her marriage. We see similar trends with Rachael and Hannah in the Bible.

Analysis

Whilst in analysis mode, you find yourself trying to rationalise: to make sense of what's going on in your world. In doing so, you may find yourself doing one or more of the following:

1. denying the facts of the situation. Both Richard and Lola had not faced up to real impact their deferred hopes were having on them

2. apportioning blame on yourself and/or others. Jason could not understand why God was taking so long in finding him a job. Rachael wondered what she had done wrong (e.g. not prayed enough) or whether there was sin in her life

3. asking questions of yourself and/or others to rationalise your predicament. For example, Richard started to question whether he had been called into the ministry at all. In the Bible, I cannot help but wonder if there were moments in Joseph's life when he wondered whether his two dreams would ever come to pass.

Despair

When in despair, everything looks bleak and gloomy, with no light at the end of the tunnel. All hope and courage seems lost. A deep sense of defeat envelops the individual, affecting their outlook on life. Jason fell into this trap when his present reality obstructed his vision of what could be a brighter future. Instead, he developed a victim 'why me?' mentality which led to self-pity.

When I think of this, the story of David and his men comes to mind. The part where their families were carried away by the Amalekites (*1 Samuel 30*). We are told that David and his men wept till they could weep no more (*1 Samuel 30:4*). Despair and grief then made David's men want to stone him. Yet, despite experiencing the same plight as his men, we are told that David found strength in the Lord his God. We are shown two different ways of handling discouragement. Both started off saddened by their loss, but David took a different approach – the God approach, which we will explore later.

The dormant phase

Words that characterise this phase include: not growing or developing; lack of advancement; temporarily inactive; a slowing down (or stopping); and being static. It is like we hang up our boots and fold our arms in one or more areas of our lives, spiritually and physically. During such times, we seem to be suspended in limbo, nursing our wounds and pain. We are neither here nor there, no longer hot or cold. We become stuck in neutral – neither moving forward or backward, until something happens to push us in either direction. If propelled in the wrong direction, over time we may find ourselves drifting further away, in particular from God. Old habits or sins may return (e.g. drinking, as we saw in Richard's case) and we end up with other issues to deal with.

Anger

Anger can set in as a result of a concoction of feelings we experience, such as:

- feeling hard-done-by – as, for instance, when we have had an injustice done to us ('it's not fair')

- not getting the answers to our searching questions ('why me?'; 'why did God allow that to happen?'; 'does He care?')

- not being able to make sense of the situation ('I don't understand; 'how could this have happened?')

- being disappointed about the situation ('after all the effort I put into it…')

- feeling helpless or that our hands are tied ('there is nothing I can do')

Richard, the aspiring preacher, exemplified this emotion where he felt an injustice had been done to him by his pastor, whom he felt was using him instead of releasing him into his own ministry. He felt that God had gone silent on him, although he had felt 'the call' in years past. The situation did not make sense to Richard and so we see bitter disappointment and anger showing up.

In addition to anger which we may direct at others, we can also experience self-directed anger when we feel we have allowed certain situations to happen or have put ourselves in a situation. 'If only I had done this … this would not have happened' is a familiar thought pattern at these times.

Withdrawing

During such times, we could find ourselves pulling away – retreating physically, spiritually, or emotionally. This can include:

- pulling away from God: Richard, Lola, Rachael and Jason did this in one shape or another

- isolating oneself from others: Lola's strategy was to throw herself into her work; Jason retreated into a 'cave'; and in the Bible, Tamar remained desolate in her brother Absalom's house after being raped and abandoned by her half brother, Amnon (*2 Samuel 13:1-22*)

- letting go of previous dreams or desires: Lola gave up on the idea of marrying the man of her dreams

- emotionally disconnecting (from activities, roles, responsibilities or relationships): Richard showed up at church all right but his heart was no longer in it. Moreover, he adopted a negative coping behaviour – drinking

I believe, if done correctly, withdrawing or retreating can be an effective way of dealing with our personal situations. However, the aim is not to isolate ourselves indefinitely. And it does not have to be done in complete isolation (unless there is a particular need for it and with assistance available when needed). For example, you can spend time in a retreat centre praying, reading, and thinking whilst surrounded by individuals who are on hand to support you (e.g. intercessors, counsellors and the like).

Becoming stuck

When stuck, we seem to become dormant and the drive to 'keep fighting' ebbs away. This can be due to:

- exhaustion from our battles: such as we see in the case of Elijah (*1 Kings 19*).

- developing a nonchalant attitude: 'What's the point?' – seeing that previous efforts did not achieve the desired results. This was an attitude developed by Lola

- not knowing which way to turn, the next step to take or how to retrace our steps: Rachael and Jason exhibited this trait

During such times, we may develop issues with God and/or find ourselves questioning our faith. In so doing, we may curtail or stop our routine spiritual activities such as praying, Bible reading, and attending church. This will contribute to the fires of our hearts gradually being extinguished though we may be unaware of this until further down the line.

As you can imagine, our 'issues' with God ultimately affect our spiritual development and may spill over into our other relationships. An example of this can be issues around trusting God. The chances are that if we struggle with trusting God, we will struggle with trusting people too.

However, despite feeling stuck, we can in fact make a u-turn – an upward turn into the hopeful phase. To do this requires the following:

1. Recognising the fact that we are discouraged.

2. Allowing others access into our 'world' (i.e. God and others).

3. Having the right level of support we need (e.g. unconditional love, compassion, comfort, a listening ear, a shoulder to cry on).

4. Becoming open and receptive to support and encouragement.

5. the determination, or self-motivation, to move beyond discouragement – demonstrated by our attitudes and behaviours.

6. Recognising our need of God's help before, during and after our encounters with discouragement.

Both positive external and internal influences can trigger a positive response. In the absence of these and/or in the presence of negative influences, we may remain stuck here (always excepting divine intervention, of course).

The hopeful phase

I believe this is the phase where we allow the rays of God's light into our troubled hearts. It is when we go through the process of facing up to our personal situation with a view of moving on. Please note that the acceptance of our personal situation does not mean becoming defeated, losing hope or giving up. It means facing up to the reality of the situation we are faced with, trusting that God still has a plan for our lives.

This means that, for example, although Rachael may mourn over her failed fertility treatment she can rise up confidently from her bathroom floor (metaphorically speaking) and face her tomorrows, knowing God is by her side and that He loves her. And Jason, though saddened that he remains jobless and unable to provide for his family, can muster up the strength to keep job searching whilst receiving government benefits, confidently assured that God will meet his needs and that God's plans for his career will unfold in time. For all of us, it means confronting our fears too (something we will look at later) and buying into the fact that 'the King still has one more move'. Simply put, it ain't over!

Acceptance

Acceptance happens when we start coming to terms with our present reality and is crucial to moving forward. Instead of feeling defeated we accept the situation and look for a way to navigate through it.

Let's take an example: you find yourself in a paddling boat, in the middle of a lake, which springs a leak. Now, you can sit there in denial thinking all will be well whilst your boat gradually fills up with water. Alternatively, you can quickly accept the fact that you are sinking, declaring, 'Houston, we have a problem!'. Now that you've admitted it, you can decide (hastily, I might add) on your plan of action. You might, for example, bail the water out yourself, cry for help to other nearby boats, or swim ashore whilst praying for a miracle. (P.S.: expecting a miracle does not mean being passive.) You've moved to take positive action to overcome the situation.

Therefore, part of our acceptance process has to

embrace the following, in order for us to move on:

- accepting God's sovereignty over all situations. At times, we lose sight of Gods power whilst focusing on our 'sinking boats'. When this is happens, we can end up: fighting against Him; not enlisting His help; or even failing to recognise other forms of help or outcomes He brings our way

- admitting to ourselves the real situation. (i.e. our boat is sinking and it may drag us down with it if we don't do anything about it.)

- recognising the impact of our 'sinking boat' trauma on us – physically, spiritually, and emotionally – and on the people around us. Often, we fail to realise the severity of the impact our life experiences have on us and the toll they take

- recognising our own limitations. For example, we might not be able to bail ourselves out of our sinking boat, which means we need the assistance of God and others

- employing our reservoirs of strength and character (e.g. resilience, determination, and deep-seated faith in God). I believe we all have a measure of this. David tapped into his reservoirs and was able to encourage himself in the Lord, despite his situation being dire and the fact that he was surrounded by people in the same position who weren't doing likewise. He then took action by seeking God and pursuing his enemies

- accepting the fact that, although our boats may have sunk once before, it is not a reason for our not getting in a boat again. Simply put: our hopes and dreams do not have to go down with the boat. It is all about rising above the situation – and the tools we use to do this are our hearts and minds.

Take on board these few points and you are ready for the next step.

Grieving

Once we have become honest with ourselves regarding the reality of our situation, there is a chance we may experience 'double-dip' sadness. At this point, after having been through the initial S.A.D. phase, we seem to plunge into another bout. However, unlike the earlier episode of sadness which occurs prior to our coming to terms with the situation, this is where we allow ourselves to go through a period of true grief over our loss, hardship, pain or trauma.

As you can imagine, this stage requires the love and comfort of God and others to pull us through, lest we find ourselves stuck and unable to move forward. A classic example of remaining stuck is Tamar (*2 Samuel 13*) who remained 'bitter and desolate'. I often wonder what became of her after her 'sinking boat' trauma. Was she able to move on with her life? Did she ever let another man touch her, let alone get married? Although she was living in the house of her brother Absalom, did she find support there? We can only make a guess as no further information is provided. However, it is easy to see how our grief can remain long after the event.

Hope

At this point, we start to see the light at the end of the tunnel. Over a period of time, our outlook moves from doom and gloom to a brighter one. I believe this comes as a result of our acceptance and grieving. Now it feels like we get new breath of wind beneath our wings. Here we are more receptive to the grace and love of God, and that of others. We seem to move away from the victim mindset to that of victor. Thanks be to God.

It is worth bearing in mind that our becoming hopeful is not necessarily the result of getting what we want (although God can do that). Referring back to the sinking boat scenario: it is not just that feeling one gets when we see the lifeguards approaching – it is about our inner confidence that everything will be fine, even in the face of adversity. This goes beyond what we see or even know. Faith is not based on what we can see but on what we cannot.

This fresh outlook and newfound hope often gets us back into gear, propelling us back into the race. If we take Jason as an example, we can see that, with the support and encouragement of others (e.g. family, church, friends, coach, etc.), he can resume his job-hunting, hopeful that something will turn up soon. He may change his strategy and consider seeking God's will for this season of his life. It could be that God is trying to focus Jason's attention on a new direction. Reassurance from his wife that she appreciates his efforts to provide for their family would help alleviate the pressure he is feeling to 'be the man'. He could appoint a friend as a coach and prayer partner – someone to whom he feels comfortable opening up.

He may learn not to take his rejections personally, accepting that firstly, he is special to God and secondly, that God has a plan for him – a plan to give him hope and a future (*Jeremiah 29:11*). And of course, with God, the future is always bright. We just have to wait to see how it all unfolds.

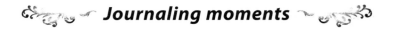 Journaling moments

Upon reading the different phases of discouragement, consider the following:

1. Would you say you are presently discouraged? If so, what makes you think so?

2. What has brought on the feeling of discouragement you are presently experiencing?

3. Which phase do you think you are at? What do you feel able to do to move to the 'hope' phase?

UNDERSTANDING THE PHASES OF DISCOURAGEMENT

PART 2

PREPARING FOR YOUR JOURNEY

Chapter 3

Spiritual truths about God

'For I am the Lord who heals you.'
(Exodus 15:26, NLT)

God is still God!

'For the word of the Lord holds true, and we can trust everything he does.' (*Psalm 33:4, NLT*)

You may not want to hear this, but God is still God – regardless of what you are experiencing or how you are feeling. Maybe you were holding on to a promise, a word, or a dream that had you utterly convinced. And then you felt let down because things did not work out the way you thought they would – just like Rachael's failed fertility treatment or Richard's aspirations to become a pastor some day. Fifteen and ten years down the line respectively, Rachael and Richard were still waiting for their dreams to become a reality. Yet, does this make God less of a God? Does the fact that God answers our prayers prove to us that He is God?

The answer is 'no' to both questions. Regardless of the situation, God is *still* God. And He does not have to prove Himself to anyone. Hence, the challenge we face is keeping His awesomeness constantly in mind, even when we are in the deepest pits of despair. It really is about keeping God magnified.

I know what effects bitter disappointment and grief can have on us. Trust me, at such times, I honestly don't feel like bringing out my tambourine and offering a sacrifice of praise – although I do. The very word 'sacrifice' is significant. To me, this is about surrendering or foregoing my personal feelings whilst offering praise to the One worthy of receiving it. And so my sacrifice will cost me something. Why? Because God is still God. I may not have what I want or be where I want to be, but can I dig deep to find one reason to praise Him.

Whilst reflecting on this, I pondered on the life of David. I came to the conclusion that he had earned the title of being a man after God's heart because He had learned this secret. No matter how depressed David became or how much complaining he did, he always found a reason to adulate and worship God. Despite the trials he was facing I could just see God's heart swell as He was being honoured. My instinct is that this may have contributed to David's finding favour with God and receiving eternal promises from Him.

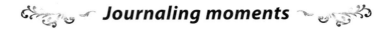 *Journaling moments*

Can you find one reason to worship God today?

God never abandons His own

> 'I once was young, now I'm a graybeard – not once have I seen an abandoned believer, or his kids out roaming the streets.' (*Psalm 37:25, MSG*)

There may be times in your journey when it feels like God has abandoned you. It might seem like God has gone on vacation and turned off His phone. However, the truth remains that God is a faithful God and He has proven this throughout time. In fact, He is the one person we can count on until the very end because that is His nature.

On my personal journey, I have learned never to rely on my feelings. The fact that I feel alone is not an indication that I am alone. God is always closer than we actually think. And so, when our senses and minds start to play tricks on us, we should remind ourselves of what His Words say because this is our eternal assurance. It is akin to checking the wording of our insurance policies to find out what is included, in the event of a crisis happening. Likewise, we need to glance through the Bible and remind ourselves of His eternal promises to us. Scriptures like *Deuteronomy 31:8* serve as great reminders:

'And the LORD, He is the One who goes before you. He will be with you, He will not leave you nor forsake you; do not fear nor be dismayed.' (*NLT*)

And so, when we are having a 'I feel alone' moment, we can be comforted by those words: 'He will not leave you nor forsake you.'. If, sometimes, we exclude ourselves from God's promises, remember that this applies to us all. How comforting to know that, although others may abandon us, God will never do so. Our challenge, in our pressing moments, is to never lose sight of such promises. Moreover, although it might feel like God is being silent or not acting the way we expect, this doesn't mean that He has abandoned us.

Journaling moments

Take some time to meditate on Isaiah 43:2–3.

Whenever you feel alone or afraid, remind yourself of this scripture.

'When you're in over your head, I'll be there with you. When you're in rough waters, you will not go down. When you're between a rock and a hard place, it won't be a dead end – Because I am God, your personal God, The Holy of Israel, your Saviour.'
(*MSG*)

Enlightening moments

If you have ever thought that God has turned His back on you, picture this: there was an enemy approaching you. God got up and stood between you and the advancing enemy. And, in that moment, His back was turned to you. But He only did this so He could fight your battles for you. This is what the Great Shepherd does for us. And, whilst you might be scared for a moment, He has certainly got your back.

God hears! God answers! But not always in the way you expect!

'True, God made everything beautiful in itself and in its time – but he's left us in the dark, so we can never

> know what God is up to, whether he's coming
> or going.'
> (*Ecclesiastes 3:11, MSG*)

The fact is, God hears all our prayers and cries from the heart, both audible and inaudible. At times, He answers them in ways our human minds cannot fathom. God is multidimensional, working in ways we cannot always discern or understand. And, because we only have what I will call a one-dimensional perspective, we get stuck, focused only on what we perceive to be the answer.

Let's take a real-life scenario – the subject of singleness. Like Lola, you might have prayed, fasted, attended conferences, been through deliverance, read books, confessed scriptures and pretty much covered all the bases. Yet there is no man in sight and your biological clock seems to ticking even louder of late. But that's fine because you know someone who got married at forty-five. And, after all, in the Bible, Sarah had Isaac at ninety. So, maybe you will become a modern day Sarah. Whilst you might be focusing on this one possibility, God has several options up His sleeve. You might be thinking of option 'a', 'b', or 'c', while God is working in combinations of 'AD', 'XYZ', 'ZYAB', or even 'JLKMN'. Get the drift?

One thing I have come to realise is that God may take different avenues to arrive at the relevant destination (i.e. marriage) or He may even use the same avenue (i.e. singleness) to arrive at altogether different destinations. But when we get stuck on what we know, leaving no room for God's creativity, we set ourselves up for discouragement.

The mere fact that we cannot see what God is up to shouldn't perturb us. The fact is, we only catch a glimpse (if that) of His eternal plans. Personally, I find this frustrating because I like to be in the 'know', so I can plan ahead. I have noticed that on a number of instances when I feel low, I realise I'm like a young child who keeps asking, 'Why?' and gets no answer. I get frustrated and feel like I am being left out of some heavenly plan. At times, I beg Him that if He could only show me a bit of the 'what', 'when', 'where', and 'how', I would feel better. But who am I kidding? Needless to say, it does not work.

So is there a lesson here to help us? I believe there is. We must keep on praying, in the belief that God not only hears but answers according to His will. This way, we do not lose focus nor do we get fixated on the methods God chooses to use. Maybe we also need to get to that place where we let God be God and simply say, 'Your will be done.'.

~ *Enlightening moments* ~

Are your feelings of discouragement linked to how you feel God ought to answer? If so, take a moment to consider, prayerfully, what God might want you to do. Whatever you do, don't stop praying or believing that God will answer you.

> 'Is he deaf – the one who made your ears? Is he blind – the one who formed your eyes?'
> (*Ps 94:9, NLT*)

God always has a plan!

> 'Relax, everything's going to be all right; rest, everything's coming together;
> open your hearts, love is on the way!'
> (*Jude 2, MSG*)

Accepting that God always has a plan for us can be difficult to comprehend, especially when it is not obvious there is one. But the fact is, He has a plan. Moreover, He is neither too early nor late (though I sometimes feel, between here and Heaven, we have an issue with the synchronisation of time – an issue I might take up with Father when I see Him!). Like

Mary and Martha when they sent word to Jesus that His friend was ill (*John, 11*), we want God to show up right now. But we all know that Jesus showed up four days after his friend's death. And, despite that, He had a plan. So this makes us question whether what seems so final in our eyes is actually final in God's. In other words, 'Can dead bones live?'

Referring back to my sinking boat scenario earlier, your strategy could be to bail out the water as fast as you can, whilst screaming for help at the top of your lungs. Yet the water keeps pouring in and is rapidly filling up the boat. In reality, the boat will sink in a matter of a few minutes and just as you are about to accept your fate (seeing as you are a non-swimmer with no lifejacket), the coastguards arrive on the scene and save you. In such situations, after thanking God, I can't help myself thinking: 'You left that a bit fine, didn't You? Why not show up sooner rather than letting me think this is it? A text message saying You are on Your way would have been nice.'

I am only joking, of course (that said, the Bible is full of messages God has kindly sent us ahead of time. So take your pick!). However, although I make light of it, I have asked God about this timing issue. And, at these times, it has helped me to think of the story of Lazarus. God did what He did to get the glory and, at the same time, He accomplished more than simply resurrecting Lazarus. The key is that there is always more to it than we can see.

We may not be able to see the bigger picture God has in mind and this is something we will struggle with on this side of glory. Hence, the likes of Lola simply come to the conclusion that it may not be God's will for her to marry. Instead, it might simply be a timing issue that just requires us to keep trusting. That is why, even though our boat may be sinking and we are running out of time, we should be careful not to leap to rash conclusions or abandon our desires. God always has a solution although it may not be what we have in mind. Was Richard born to preach? Will Lola get married before turning fifty? Will Rachael ever get pregnant? Will Jason find a job soon? Only God knows how their stories will turn out. Only one thing is for sure: God's plan for their life will come about, at the appointed time – if they allow Him in.

As He says in *Habakkuk 2:3*:

> 'For the vision is yet for an appointed time; But at the end it will speak, and it will not lie. Though it tarries, wait for it; Because it will surely come, It will not tarry.' (*NKJ*)

 *Enlightening moments*

Consider this: God had a plan for Jesus. This plan was for Jesus to die on a Cross to take away the sins of the world. Now the process of doing this would require Jesus to go through immense suffering, pain and ultimately death – all for God's plans and purposes to come to pass. Now I am not saying that you will have to die to fulfil God's plan (though some have), but if God did not spare His only begotten Son whom He loved dearly and was pleased with, why should He spare our suffering? There may come a time when you and I have to suffer an injustice, disappointment, pain and much more before the realisation of the Father's plan. This isn't an indication of God's being unfair, unjust, unkind or unfaithful. It simply is the process that He chooses to use to get things done. I know it can be hard seeing the benefit in pain and suffering. But if you were to ask Paul, David, Job, Joseph, and many others, they might just tell you it was worth it, and more.

God understands your frustrations

'For we know that all creation has been groaning as in the pains of childbirth right up to the present time. And we believers also groan, even though we have the Holy Spirit within us as a foretaste of future glory, for we long for our bodies to be released from sin and suffering...' (*Romans 8: 22-23, NLT*)

Somewhere on my journey with God, I had somehow convinced myself that He would be angry with me if I dared show any signs of discouragement, weakness, or anything I didn't consider matched up to what I felt was His desire for me. Hence, my aim was to be strong at all times, at any cost. However, there have been times when the storms of life hit, when I have found myself sucked into the chasm of discouragement. When I realised this, I would feel guilty for letting God down, like a soldier who broke rank (albeit for good reason). With my soul in a state of unrest – having, on one side, feelings of guilt and on the other, discouragement – I found myself thinking, 'I shouldn't be feeling this way'. But, all the while, my 'storm' seemed to be unrelenting, battering me right, left and centre.

After many episodes of discouragement and guilt, I felt God step in to break this cycle, in an unusual way. The first thing I experienced was a deep sense of compassion from Him – not the anger of a scornful father that I was expecting. It was as if He was telling me that it was okay, He understood exactly what I was going through. The fact that I wasn't prepared for this response highlighted that I really hadn't got to grips with the nature of God's love for me. Not only does God really love me but He is concerned about me and understands how life makes me feel at times.

As I was getting to grips with this unfathomable love, I felt the Spirit of God paint a picture in my mind to help me understand what I was experiencing. The picture was that of an expectant mum-to-be in the latter months of pregnancy. Even though I was excited at the joy that laid ahead – the fulfilment of my hopes, dreams and prayers – there were times when I felt weary, anxious and uncomfortable from the weight of what I was carrying. It wasn't simply a case of a nine-month gestation – I had been earnestly awaiting my delivery date for years! Before seeing God's picture, I had continued to pray and hope, but with no delivery date in sight – no indication at all of when I would 'give birth' – I had started to feel down.

Now, I finally understood why I had been feeling so weary and anxious. And, although His solution was not to provide me with a delivery date or even to 'induce' labour, what was resoundingly obvious was He was giving me His comfort to get me through to the appointed time. Being the Creator of all things, He had the power to press the 'fast forward' button (to give short term relief), but due to His fathomless understanding of timing He chose not to. Much in the way a premature birth could be detrimental, He recognised a premature spiritual birth could be just as hazardous to me, and ultimately His will. Instead, He chooses to wait with me, comfort me and even carry me when my legs fail.

This experience helped me understand the scripture in 2 *Corinthians 1:3–4*:

> *'All praise to God, the Father of our Lord Jesus Christ. God is our merciful Father and the source of all comfort. He comforts us in all our troubles so that we can comfort others. When they are troubled, we will be able to give them the same comfort God has given us.' (NLT)*

God is all about comforting us through our times of trouble. This demonstrates a loving, compassionate and understanding Father. So rather than beat yourself up for feeling the way you do, isn't it time you experience His true love towards you? God understands our earthly plights and is always on hand through the Holy Spirit – our Comforter – to see us through.

In closing this section, please note this is not a license to remain discouraged. Rather, it serves to remind us that we are not in this alone in our journey. God understands and so we can come before Him, tell Him how we feel and receive comfort.

Enlightening moments

Still not convinced that God understands and cares about us? Consider the following:

- He understood the heavy burden the children of Israel were under in Egypt. Hence, He sent Moses to deliver them.

- He understood the troubles of the Samarian woman. And so He sent Jesus to meet her at the well to change her life forever.

- He understood the impact of sin on man. Because of this, He sent His only Son, Jesus, to die so we can be reconciled to Him.

The Bible helps us catch a glimpse of the loving and understanding Father we have. He is not the kind to strike us off. Instead, He demonstrates His nature to us time and time again.

Chapter 4
Essential truths about life

'Many are the afflictions of the righteous,
but the LORD delivers him out of them all.'
(*Psalm 34:19, NKJ*)

Accept that life happens

'Say to the righteous that it shall be well with them...'
(*Isaiah 3:10, NKJ*)

The fact is, life happens. And it can, at times, be disappointing. There are times when we are overlooked, betrayed, rejected or wronged. Dreams and desires can fail to materialise despite our best intentions and efforts. At times, we make poor decisions and unwise choices which affect us on many levels. Sometimes it seems we face endless battles and challenges, not having an opportunity to catch our breath. We experience loss and pain through sickness, accidents, death and separation. The list goes on ...

There are some Christian folk who seem to think that Christians are excluded from all this and that our journey will be a smooth ride all the way. It is like they believe we are wrapped in some form of spiritual bubble that will make us immune from life's difficulties. This was a mindset I adopted as a young Christian until I faced some serious reality checks. Whilst I truly believe that, with God on our side, we have something that separates us as His children, I have also come to recognise from scripture that life is not always plain sailing, if ever, for the believer. However, what we do have are eternal promises of our Lord to be with us when the going gets tough and bring us through (e.g. *Psalm 34:19; Isaiah 43:2*). So while we certainly don't wait for trouble or pray for it, we can be rest assured that God will be with us through it all when it shows up.

Personally, had I been taught this earlier in my Christian walk the chances are I could have avoided a number of discouraging moments. Rather than interpreting my challenges as a result of God's abandonment or my sin, I could have been more prepared for the journey ahead. With my sound understanding of God's Word and my faith in Him, I could have been prepared to handle 'life'.

I feel there is a lesson to learn here: life happens but it shall be well with us. God is in control and working all things out for our good.

Discouragement can affect anyone

'In the world you have tribulation and trials and distress and frustration; but be of good cheer [take courage; be confident, certain, undaunted!]. For I have overcome the world. [I have deprived it of power to harm you and have conquered it for you.]'
(John 16:33, AMP)

In the scripture above, we see Jesus warning us that there will be challenging and distressing times in our journey on Earth. For many of us, this is a reality we don't like to face or accept but it does not change this fact. Nonetheless, during difficult periods in our lives we may find ourselves sorrowful and discouraged.

The good news is that you are not alone in experiencing these feelings. If you were to glance through the Bible you will catch a glimpse of many who experienced discouragement. These include the likes of David, Job, Elijah, and Jeremiah. In the book of Psalms, you see David (and the other writers) express their sorrows, disappointments, thoughts and feelings to God. David, for example, experienced many challenges in his life. There was the time when the Amalekites raided Ziklag, burned it down and carried off the women, children and everyone else (*1 Samuel 30*). It was said that David and his men 'wept till they could weep no more'

(*1 Samuel 30:4*) though later David found strength in the Lord (*1 Samuel 30:6*). And this was by no means the only discouraging episode in David's life.

Elijah, the prophet, was another individual bitten by the 'discouragement bug'. He wanted God to end his life in spite of his accomplishing a great feat on Mount Carmel (*1 Kings 18–19*). Job, too, suffered great loss and hardship which he had to bear alone without support from his unhelpful friends. Out of sheer frustration, both Jeremiah and Job resented the fact they were even born (*Jeremiah 15:10; 20:14–18, Job 10:18*). Search through the Bible and you will find the accounts of many others who experienced discouragement.

But why would God choose to keep these accounts in the Bible? If He had wanted to, He could have opted to do otherwise. I believe there are many reasons for this, including:

1. To keep things real and to help us feel 'normal'. If the Bible were to omit these instances, we would struggle to relate and may draw the wrong conclusions about God, others, ourselves and life.

2. To help us learn from those who have gone ahead of us, through their responses and how they handled their situations (the good, the bad and the ugly).

3. To give us a clear insight on how God helps His children during discouraging times (e.g. He listens and meets their needs).

4. To help us through challenging and distressing times of our own. In turn, we too can encourage and comfort others.

5. To encourage us, build our confidence in God and give us hope during trying times.

6. To remind us of God's sovereign power and ability to turn situations around and bring glory to His name. Such experiences challenge our thinking as to who He really is.

7. To gain a deeper understanding of God and draw us closer to Him.

8. To help us understand that discouragement can affect anyone.

The Bible is not denying the fact that we will experience storms that might perturb us. Rather, I believe it serves to equip us for the journey ahead. In *John 16:33*, we see Jesus giving the disciples a 'heads up' on what is to come yet encouraging them to 'be of good cheer' because He has conquered the world on our behalf. So when we are discouraged, we are to remember that Christ has gone ahead of us to give us victory.

Journaling moment

Struggling with admitting to having a discouraged heart and troubled soul? Why not come clean to God today? As you may have picked up, He has not got an issue with you being open and honest. So tell Him today!

Start by making a note in your journal of where you find yourself today. List all the experiences that have discouraged or troubled you. Write down the feelings, thoughts, disappointments and fears you have had along the way.

Now bring them before God and ask Him to heal and restore you. Ask Him to help bring you along in your journey, bringing glory to His name.

Discouragement is neither a sin nor a sign of weakness!

> 'But in my distress I cried out to the Lord; yes, I prayed to my God for help.
> He heard me from his sanctuary; my cry to him reached his ears.'
> (*Psalm 18:6, NLT*)

We have already established that on our journey it is likely we will encounter distressing times. Yet, it never ceases to amaze me how much pressure we put ourselves under to act like we are strong Christians able to tough it out no matter what. Whilst I have no doubt who I am in Christ, it does not take away the fact that at some point in my Christian walk there may be situations that have the potential to discourage me. Whilst I agree that we must manage these times effectively to minimise their effect, it is only natural to feel down because we are human.

The reality is that many of us keep the lid firmly on our emotions, suppressing the anguish of our hearts. In not acknowledging the naturalness of some of our human reactions to challenging situations we bring on ourselves further difficulties. We seem to believe that showing the signs of discouragement is a sign of weakness or even a sin. But answer this: is it a sin to feel down when we lose a loved one? Is it a sign of weakness to cry when a tragedy occurs? If your answer is 'yes' then you have just declared Jesus a sinner and weak. Did Jesus not cry when Lazarus, His beloved friend, died? (*John 11:35*). Was Jesus not said to be troubled and deeply distressed as the hour of His death on the cross loomed closer? (*Mark 14:33–34; Matthew 26:37–38*). Do either of these situations make Jesus a sinner or weak? I believe you will agree with me that the answer is 'no'. So why do we make ourselves or others feel bad about feeling discouraged during hard times? We would hardly expect one to rejoice after getting the news of a close family member or friend dying. Would we not count it strange if an individual had just been diagnosed with terminal cancer and they left their doctor dancing?

I believe this idea of needing to appear almost superhuman (or abnormal, if you ask me!) stems from taking scriptures out of context. For instance, I have heard people preach about *Proverbs 24:10* which states,

> 'If you faint in the day of adversity, Your strength is small.' (*NKJ*)

They have interpreted these words to suggest we have

to get a grip — or else we are just some weaklings of Christians who are obviously not sufficiently grounded in God. I have to admit that, for a time, I tacitly bought into this notion — after all, I'd heard it often enough. Now I realise that, although this scripture can be used to emphasize the need to develop spiritual muscle to help us withstand the storms of life, it does not mean that we shouldn't cry or express any signs of distress when we are in the thick of it. Moreover, I believe the scripture captures one simple point: Don't give up!

I had well-meaning Christians tell me to be strong when I lost my father. I appreciate we are often at loss as to what to say in times of bereavement but it is only natural to feel melancholic, especially through the early stages of grief. Personally, I feel that trying to appear strong only prolonged my grieving period. I had never lost anyone close before and here I was, tussling with the need to appear as if I was handling it, although the reality was that I was falling apart on the inside. Dealing with grief was not something I had been taught in university, nor had church prepared me for the emptiness I would carry around inside me for many years. Was I really weak or was I just being normal? Looking back, I know for sure that my natural inner struggles were in conflict with the mindsets I had picked up along the way. This kept me in the 'dormant' phase, we discussed earlier, for a long time.

It took God to get me out of the cycle by helping me understand that it was normal to grieve, cry and feel down in certain situations. And, when He felt the time was right for me, He gently took me by the hand, helped me back on my feet and told me it was time to move on. I can't exactly pinpoint an exact time or date when my 'dormant' phase was over, all I know is that at some point I realised that I was no longer carrying the heavy weight of grief in my heart because I had moved on to the next stage, the hopeful stage. He had turned my mourning into dancing.

 *Enlightening moment*

Uplifting moments as shared by David in *Psalm 30:11–12*:

'You did it: you changed wild lament into whirling dance;
You ripped off my black mourning band and decked me with wildflowers.
I'm about to burst with song; I can't keep quiet about you.
God, my God, I can't thank you enough.' (*MSG*)

Trials have an expiry date!

'Weeping may last through the night, but joy comes with the morning.'
(*Psalm 30:5, NLT*)

All trials and challenging situations – those 'storms of life' – have an end date. Nothing lasts forever, not even this life as we know it. For there will come a time when Jesus will reappear in the Second Coming of Christ. And, with this in mind, we are helped to keep things in perspective, although this can be difficult at times. Our challenges have nothing to do with eternity with Christ and everything to do with what happens in the running up to it. And it is these present day challenges that get us down, which you can see in the stories of Richard, Lola, Rachael and Jason. Yes, life can be hard sometimes – but nothing can take away the fact that it will all come to pass.

When I reflect on the notion of trials, I always look back to the life of Jesus. From what I understand in the Bible (e.g. *Isaiah 53*), dying on the cross was not exactly a walk in the park nor was His three-year ministry, come to think of it. Yet, in spite of everything, He forged ahead. I often wonder how Jesus coped, especially when the people He was dying for did not appreciate Him. (After all, any of us will get disheartened at times we don't feel appreciated.) In Jesus' case, He wasn't just unappreciated, He was rejected and despised as well. Often, I find myself trying to step into His shoes to understand His thoughts and feelings. I frequently scour the Gospels to shed a light on His coping strategies. (The most fundamental was a close relationship with God.)

More often than not, I find myself asking Him prayerfully to give me the wisdom and strength to plough on, even when it seems *everything* is against me, so that I too can accomplish what Father wants to do in my life. To do this means pushing past what I see or experience. For me to bear my cross, I need to adopt the essential attitudes, beliefs and behaviours that will keep me going to the end.

One day, a particular insight hit me: *Jesus kept eternity in mind*. By doing this, looking beyond His own hurt and pain, He persevered through to the cross so that mankind would be saved (*Philippians 2*). The question for me was whether I too was willing to carry my cross, in whatever shape or form it came, for eternity's sake.

You may not see the eternal relevance or even purpose of your personal challenges right now, but there is one.

Ecclesiastes 3:11, which I have mentioned before, says:

'He has made everything beautiful in its time. Also He has put eternity in their hearts, except that no one can find out the work that God does from beginning to end.' (*NKJ*)

You may not be able to see the full extent of what God is doing but we need to keep in mind that He has 'planted eternity in our hearts', no matter what. Am I saying this will be easy? Absolutely not! However, I am confident that if we embrace this mindset, along with a close relationship with God and others, we will be okay. The key point to always keep in mind is that trials have an expiry date – they don't last forever.

Enlightening moment

'We've been surrounded and battered by troubles, but we're not demoralized; we're not sure what to do, but we know that God knows what to do; we've been spiritually terrorized, but God hasn't left our side; we've been thrown down, but we haven't broken.'
(*2 Corinthians 4:8–9, MSG*)

Help is always available

'Meanwhile, the moment we get tired in the waiting, God's Spirit is right alongside helping us along.'
(Romans 8:26. MSG)

When we feel down, as a result of going through a trial, we often believe that we are alone and helpless. This could be as a result of actually being abandoned by others – pretty much how Paul would have felt in 2 Timothy 4:16–18 – or we simply feel like it, although it may not be the reality.

However, wherever we find ourselves today, one thing of which I am convinced is that God always makes provision during such times. Going back to Paul's experience: he made a profound statement that has stuck with me till today. He said:

'But the Lord stood with me and gave me strength so that I might preach the Good News in its entirety for all the Gentiles to hear.' (NLT)

This tells me that help is always on hand to guide us through our most difficult times. It was the same help that was available to Shadrach, Meshach, and Abednego (Daniel 3) when God showed up in the fiery furnace.

Or when God sent angels to shut the mouths of the lions when Daniel was thrown in the lions den (*Daniel 6*). Or when He led the children of Israel victoriously out of Egypt after hearing their cries (*Exodus 12–14*). And when He gave David victory over Goliath (*1 Samuel 17*). Or when He sent an angel to Hagar when He heard the cries of little Ishmael in the wilderness (*Genesis 21*).

Throughout time, God has shown up in various ways and, before Jesus left the earth, He gave us the Holy Spirit. The amplified version of the Bible calls Him 'the Comforter' – as well as Counselor, Helper, Intercessor, Advocate, Strengthener, and Standby (*John 14:16*). Have you noticed that these words describe Someone who can help us in every major life situation we may face? The Holy Spirit is on hand to help in many ways and we need to embrace this fact. And remember, just when you feel you can't go on and it looks all doom and gloom, you have Someone fighting your corner. He will give you 'wind beneath your wings' to uplift you from within. It is the same Holy Spirit that will pray on our behalf in our moments of weakness when all we are able to do is sigh (*Romans 8:26*). What a relief to know that, whether people show up or not to help me, I have Someone who has got my back and will help me through!

 *Journaling moment*

Study *Romans 8:18–28* (preferably in the *Message* Bible version). What messages of hope can you glean from this scripture?

ESSENTIAL TRUTHS ABOUT LIFE

PART 3

STRATEGIES TO DEVELOP AN ENCOURAGED HEART

Chapter 5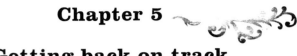

Getting back on track

'Forgetting the past and looking forward to what lies ahead ...'
(*Philippians 3:13, NLT*)

In order for you to move forward from discouragement, there some mental shifts you will need to make. The first is a determination, on your part, to want to move on. It is one thing saying this, but quite another actually getting your head and heart around it. If these crucial parts of you don't buy into the idea, 'moving on' simply becomes part of a wish list – and is something you're unlikely to act on. Just remember: your attitudes and beliefs underpin your behaviours.

The second thing you will need to do as you embark on this part of the book is to step back from blaming anyone or anything – be it God, others, life, or even yourself. Blame does nothing but hold you back from receiving the healing your heart so much needs. It becomes an obstacle to your being able to receive all that God has in mind for you. It is almost as though you need to change the lenses you look through so that you can see clearly and have a different outlook. If not, all you will continue to see is how you were wronged or hurt. Please note this is in no way aimed at belittling your experiences or denying them. Rather, try and see it as you being thrown a lifeline after being trapped in quicksand. The priority is to get out before it suffocates you. Once out, you can then analyse the situation to establish how you got stuck there in the first place.

The third thing you will need to do is to act on what you read. Unless you act, you won't see the changes you desire. Taking action, especially when it is unfamiliar and we have to break new ground, can be challenging. It requires effort, as there is a good chance that we might have to change our behaviour or learn a new one. However, sticking with what is comfortable or what feels safe may not get you to your destination – a hopeful heart. So you will need to take action, albeit baby steps.

If you don't adopt these mental shifts you may find yourself going round in circles without actually moving forward. This is certainly not my desire for you and my prayer is that God will change the way you think so you can experience His fullness of joy.

The God factor

'… In Your presence is fullness of joy …' (*Psalm 16:11, NKJ*)

Get God onboard

This is all about enlisting God's help in dealing with your discouraged heart and your troubled soul. It might seem like the obvious thing to do, especially as a Christian. However, I have come to realise that knowing what to do and actually doing it are completely different things. We might say it with our mouths but unless it has it sunk deep into our hearts we won't be nudged into action.

Invite Him in

Getting God onboard can happen in many ways but you need to start by inviting Him into the situation. The key thing is to recognise that we are not able to move forward without His help. It is akin to a young child asking its parent for help when they are struggling with a task, such as tying a shoe lace or getting something that is out of reach. We can imagine ourselves as children grappling with a difficult task, in this case the struggle is with our discouraged heart, something we definitely need God's help with. And so, the initial step is about coming to Him and asking for His help.

Through this process, we are admitting His sovereignty over all matters. By approaching His throne we are recognising that without His help we will continue to struggle with this burden in our heart. In seeking God, we are affirming His lordship over our lives and this is an important tool in developing our relationship with Him. And if this has dwindled, for whatever reason, or we have gone our own way, it gives us the opportunity to mend the relationship and bridge the gap – just as the prodigal son did when he went straight into the arms of his loving father.

Become open and honest

Bringing Father into the situation allows us to be open and honest with Him about our thoughts, feelings, hurts and pains. Not that He was unaware of them, but there is something deeply therapeutic and liberating when one offloads ones burdens onto Him. We all know what it feels like to be listened to and sensing the feeling of being heard. The only difference is that in talking to God, we are sharing our hearts with the Creator of the universe – the One who can do and undo. We can confidently bring our case to Him knowing He will be unbiased yet loving. Compassionate yet fair. There isn't a judgemental streak in Him and, even if He shows us the errors of our ways, 'He can tell you off without actually feeling you have been told off!' as a friend of mine put it. And when we pray and study His Word, we will start to grow and somehow find ourselves moving on.

Personally, it took me many years to bring the 'matters of my heart' to Him. Whilst I had no qualms calling upon Him to help me with a financial need or when I was unwell – or even with a small favour like helping me find my lost my keys – it was a challenge to bring to His presence the issues that plagued my heart. Over the years, I have noticed this in the lives of the women I've worked with. It should not surprise me because it all started with Adam and Eve in the Bible who felt the need to hide themselves from God after being deceived by the serpent. Today, we are still trying to hide ourselves from God, hoping to keep from Him our true states – which, of course, is impossible.

Deal with trust issues

'Trust God from the bottom of your heart; don't try
to figure out everything on your own.
Listen for God's voice in everything you do,
everywhere you go ...'
(*Proverbs 3:5–6, MSG*)

Although we may claim with our mouths that we trust God, in actual fact, our hearts – and consequently our behaviours – betray us. As someone who has had her fair share of discouragement, I admit that it is, at times, difficult to *really* trust God when you feel He no longer warrants that trust. When we feel let down by God we struggle to trust Him. Reflecting back on the stories I shared earlier, all the individuals I described felt God had let them down and this affected their subsequent reactions. Take, for instance, Richard who started to resent God and took to drinking. Then there was Lola who gave up on the idea of getting married. Rachael could not fathom why her prayers seemed to be falling on deaf ears and Jason could not understand why it was taking so long to get a job so that he could provide for his family. Their situation made them start to question their trust in God and His ability to deliver on His promises, although they did not necessarily vocalise this.

While in this frame of mind, can you categorically

say you trust God? Can you confidently come before Him, pour out your heart to Him about your situation and ask for His help? The chances are you may struggle with this because, if you are anything like me and other humans, you may get so focused on God's outstanding to-do list regarding your life that you completely miss the fact that He is still God. Trusting God through the hard times can be hard but it is still required of us. And so, we need help in reframing our minds and focusing on who God is. When I struggle with this, I find that revisiting His Word and reminding myself of His great feats in the Bible helps a lot. Taking a trip down memory lane in my life works wonders too. Although I may be fixated on the huge mountain before me, when I reflect on some of the mountains He has actually moved out of my way in the past I soon find myself repenting at His feet. How could I forget the great things He has done so far? Does this situation now make Him less of who He is? No!

I remember one time when I was having a moaning session in God's presence I felt Him say to me, 'Don't base your impression of Me on what is going on in your life right now – what you have or don't have – but base it on who I *am*'. This certainly jerked the slack out of me. It was as if He was a good God when He did what I wanted and less so when things did not go my way. Oh Lord help us all!

Please note this is not to make you feel guilty. Rather, it is to make you aware of how you might be responding to God. Many of us have moments like we see in *Psalm 73:13* where the writer rants:

'Is it in vain I kept my heart pure?' (*NLT*)

But we too can conclude, as the writer does in verse 26 of the same chapter:

'My health may fail, and my spirit may grow weak, but God remains the strength of my heart; he is mine forever.' (*NLT*)

Let go and let God

'Yet I am confident I will see the Lord's goodness while I am here in the land of the living.'
(*Psalm 27:13, NLT*)

There was a game we used to play in school where you had to close your eyes and fall backwards so that a group of friends could catch you. Participation in this game was based on the premise that your friends were able to catch you – that they got your back. It felt good allowing myself to relax and free-fall into the safe arms of my friends.

This is how we ought to be with God – confident of His capable arms. Although we can't see Him, we must trust that He has 'got our backs' too – be it through the good or bad times. Until we get past this we will keep acting like God is clumsy, not up to the task or simply preoccupied with catching others. We are forgetting scriptures like *Psalm 121:4* that says:

'He never slumbers nor sleeps.' (*NLT*)

Or *Isaiah 40:28* that says:

'He never grows weak nor weary.' (*NLT*)

Yet, somewhere deep inside us, we conclude that God can't or won't be there when we need Him. I find it helpful to think of it as the need to change our lenses, something I mentioned earlier. If we keep looking through the wrong lenses of life – at past disappointments, incorrect mindsets, doubt, etc. – we may fail to see God's arms stretched out towards us, especially if our backs are turned to Him and our focus is elsewhere. In short, we don't see all He is capable of.

This section reminds me of my early years as a 'real' Christian. I remember that getting answers to prayers was relatively easy – I did not even have to ask. At times, all it took was a mere thought (as it describes in *Isaiah 65:24*), and what I wanted came to pass. However, as the years rolled by, it seemed that this had stopped working for me. I realised I had to change tactics: get more serious with my prayer life. And, even with this, after a while it felt like God was not working fast enough to clear my backlog of prayers.

So I changed my strategy yet again. This time, I took full control of the reins of my life – or, rather, I snatched them out of Gods hands. I did this because I no longer trusted that He would 'catch' me or be there for me. I was looking through the lens of 'God has let me down'. It was like my friends hadn't caught me, in the game I mentioned earlier. They'd let me fall and now there was no way I was playing it again with them. This was my attitude towards God too at that stage.

A challenge we face as Christians is, when we are not sure if God has our back covered, that we resort into trying to figure things out by ourselves. We no longer allow God the opportunity to work fully in our lives. And so we create a stumbling block to our own progress. Of course, when we are exhausted with fighting our own battles, when things don't work out or when we come to the end of ourselves, discouragement may creep in. Therefore, I encourage you to consider whether you need to let go of whatever it is and hand it over to God fully.

 Journaling moment

Opening up to God

We all have ways we like to talk to God. So find your way of communicating your present challenges and sorrows. Suggestions for this can include:

- telling Him verbally (in prayer)
- writing it in the form of a letter (*Dear God ...*)
- finding a song, picture, or other forms of art that communicate how you feel

Allow yourself adequate time and go with the flow. Ultimately, your aim is to unload your burdens onto Him.

Chapter 6
Digging deeper beyond your unmet need

'Don't copy the behaviour and customs of this world, but let God transform you into a new person by changing the way you think.'
(*Romans 12:2, NLT*)

Deal with your mind

'Summing it all up, friends, I'd say you'll do best by filling your minds and meditating on things true, noble, reputable, authentic, compelling, gracious – the best, not the worst; the beautiful, not the ugly; things to praise, not things to curse. Put into practice what you learned from me, what you heard and saw and realized. Do that, and God, who makes everything work together, will work you into his most excellent harmonies.'
(*Philippians 4:8–9, MSG*)

God has given each of us the responsibility of managing our own mind. This includes developing and nurturing it. Part of this includes controlling what we feed it with as this has a direct consequence on what comes out. In short, our actions are underpinned by our beliefs which feed off what we put into our minds. And so if you allow garbage in, you will get garbage out. Without proper control, this could become a vicious cycle of which we struggle to get out. We need to ensure that we are cultivating healthy minds and mindsets by feeding on nourishing foods such as God's Word. You really can't beat that.

This same notion is true when it comes to our state of mind before, during and after discouraging times. If you fortify yourself regularly with God's Word, you end up strengthening yourself. Whilst this may not completely immunise you from the effects of difficult life events, your recovery will be quicker and you may not react to them as adversely as someone who has not fortified themselves at all. Without this special nourishment, we may find ourselves falling in a heap on the wayside at the very first sign of trouble and utterly losing hope.

If you are struggling with discouragement take a moment to consider your state of mind running up to the situation, or situations, that caused it. Could you have invested more to prevent it taking hold? Did your efforts in fortifying yourself start to wane although you started off well? Believe me when I say

I'm not casting aspersions: many of us have struggled with discouragement – I know how it is. However, this chapter is all about looking under every stone to help us not only learn more about ourselves but empower us to take the necessary action. This way we'll be taking steps to deal with our discouraged hearts and troubled souls.

Let us take this scenario: if all you see is doom and gloom or the cup being half empty – and even some of us Christians find this the case – sooner or later you will find yourself migrating towards a depressive state. Meditate on such thoughts long enough, without pulling yourself self out of it, and you can become stuck. Hence, we have to take a proactive stance and use the Word of God as a filtering mechanism. That way we can keep out what might be trying to sneak in without our knowing, trying to make its home in our minds. These gloomy thoughts can end up weakening us, without our realising it, and may show up in our response to trying times.

Watch out for seeds of doubt

During hard times, we need to keep our gazes heavenward and resist looking around us. Maintaining this concentration can be hard at times but is not impossible. When Peter moved his focus to the strong wind and waves he was no longer able to walk on water. Instead, he started to sink. Up until that point, when his gaze had been fixed squarely on Jesus, he was fine (*Matthew 14:22-33*).

At times, like Peter, we get distracted. We start off well, battling adversity head-on, embarking on our own 'walking on water' experiences. Then, all of a sudden, something else grabs our attention and we become fixated on it. It starts off as a seed in our minds. When I think of Peter, I can imagine him starting to walk towards Jesus' outstretched hand, thinking, 'Wow, this is so cool. I am actually walking on water'. Then, just before he began to sink, his 'wow' moment moved to: 'Hold on a minute, this is not possible!' and 'Oh my God, that ten-foot wave is coming right at me and I've only just started swimming lessons. What am I going to do? Someone help! Call the lifeguards!"'. Laugh you may, but Peter's story is a very good illustration of our own predicament. Although Jesus is with us, throwing us a lifeline, somehow in times of adversity it does not seem to be enough to keep our faith levels up. Maybe our faith wavers as the idea of His being there seems impossible or surreal. But, before we know it, fear and doubt creep in.

By the way, if you read the passage, you will notice

that Jesus did not calm the storm whilst they were in the sea. In *Matthew 14:31-32* we are told that it ceased only after they had got into the boat. Now Jesus could have made life easier for Peter but if he had done could we still call this faith? If we only step out of the boat when we know it is safe to do so, many of us will fail to experience God in His fullness.

Don't let facts of the situation deter you from keeping your mind fixed on the goal

Jason, who we looked at earlier, started his job hunt on a high after being made redundant. However, he didn't remain buoyant. This was because he took his mind off the goal, concentrating instead on the following:

- fact 1 – it had been eighteen months since he had been laid off

- fact 2 – he had been rejected for every job he'd gone for

- fact 3 – he was putting a lot of effort into his job search but not getting results

- fact 4 – he lacked the money to provide for his family and had to rely on government support

And so Jason lined up all these facts, and more, in his mind. It seemed perfectly natural to do so – they were, after all, the realities of his current situation. However, a problem arose when these 'facts' seemed to crowd out some of the biblical 'facts' he knew and held dear, so much so that they no longer resonated in his heart. In difficult times, when our present 'facts' shout the loudest they drown out everything else – like a misbehaving child getting all of the teacher's attention while little Johnny sits ignored in the corner, quietly doing what he is told. Our minds are powerful things!

Jason found himself having lost sight of God as well as the very hope of rebuilding his career and family life. Day in day out, as his mind became fixated on the 'facts', he began to lose sight of the possibility of a brighter future. If we find ourselves in this state, we too fold our arms and find ourselves drifting from our daily practices. And, even if we try to maintain them, our minds start to pose questions like: 'what's the point?' or 'is all this working?'. Ultimately, our cluttered minds, fed on a diet of doubt, fear and worry, start to affect how we act, or whether we take action at all.

Consequently, we see Jason retreating into the cave of discouragement. He never meant to end up there but it happened. He focused on what seemed to be 'true' as opposed to what was really true – that God was with him in the midst of the storm, and He could 'speak' to the situation and turn it around. We too can use this scripture, and others, to help us put things into place.

The scriptures offer us a list of things we should fill our minds with, of the right calibre. Ideas worthy of pondering on. Sadly our modern day environments tend to steer us in the opposite direction. Thanks to the media, we find ourselves with a bunch of other worries, in addition to our own. Plonked in front of the TV, soaking up all it has to offer, you will only find your discouraged heart and troubled soul further burdened. But it is not just the TV or other forms of media we should be mindful of. The people you surround yourself with can pollute your mind too. Have you ever hung around someone who has a negative outlook on life? Hang round them long enough and you start to feel and act the same. Why? Because behaviour breeds behaviour. And we need to be vigilant, not only in how we spend our time but also with whom we spend it.

Is your mind under attack?

We wrestle not only against flesh and blood but also against spiritual powers and forces of darkness (*Ephesians 6:10-12*). Because we need to be mindful of the devil's devices, we should acknowledge that discouragement can be a result of a spiritual assail of some sort. I've noticed that, on occasion, one moment you're fine and the next you find yourself down in the dumps, for no apparent reason. We have a tendency to allow these to go unnoticed, although we may try to come up with a reason. But we do need to be vigilant – don't be fooled: the enemy is always looking for something to steal, kill or destroy. And that includes your joy.

In the Bible, we see evidence of a spirit of heaviness or discouragement operating in the life of Saul (e.g. *1 Samuel 16*). This happened after he rebelled against God. In reading about Saul I couldn't help wondering if his discouragement had been fuelled by the contents of his heart and mind – wanting to look good before people rather than submitting to God, followed, later on, by feelings of insecurity and jealousy towards David. It certainly seems to be so.

Times of discouragement call for us to question the contents of hearts along with our standing with God. I believe that, when we overlook these, they do weaken us, making us more susceptible to the enemy – even though he will always try it on anyway. To help us with this, *Ephesians 6:10–12* sets out a strategy:

> 'And that about wraps it up. God is strong, and he wants you strong. So take everything the Master has set out for you, well-made weapons of the best materials. And put them to use so you will be able to stand up to everything the Devil throws your way. This is no afternoon athletic contest that we'll walk away from and forget about in a couple of hours. This is for keeps, a life-or-death fight to the finish against the Devil and all his angels.'
> (*MSG*)

It emphasizes the fact that we need to be adequately suited up so that we can resist our spiritual assailants. Moreover, it is not something we do every now and then but daily.

Train your mind

It is just not good enough professing to know something – you need to put it into practice. Regardless of where you are on the continuum of encouragement and discouragement, the bottom line is that you will need to put on your whole armour. *Ephesians 6:13–18* suggests a number of actions we can take:

- building a lifestyle founded on truth, integrity, moral rectitude and right-standing with God

- learning to be at peace, uplifted, grounded and unshakeable through the Good News

- using your faith as a shield against challenging and perturbing situations

- fighting your battles using God's Words along with the power and authority you have as a believer

- praying in the spirit at all times. It is essential

- keeping your spiritual radar on and being alert

- praying not only for yourself but for other brothers and sisters in the Lord, so that no-one drops out of the race

These are actions you need to maintain for the rest of your life, not just as a one-off. To accomplish this, the Word of God is our starting point which we can use to nourish, develop, heal and purge our minds. In the case of the latter, 2 *Corinthians 10:5* suggests:

> 'We destroy every proud obstacle that keeps people from knowing God. We capture their rebellious thoughts and teach them to obey Christ.'
> (*NLT*)

I believe this goes for believers and unbelievers though we tend to use it in prayer for salvation. We too need to stand against anything that keeps us from knowing and experiencing God fully – and that includes that 'stuff' we find floating about in our minds. We must train our minds to align themselves with the standards the Bible has set us.

Strategies like the mentioned above can get left on the back-burner owing to our busy and cluttered lives. It might be worth making a mental note – or one in your diary or calendar – to check in with how your mind is doing. Your aim is to run a diagnostic check on what is going on in your mind. If we were to put a microphone there, what messages, thoughts and belief-systems would we hear? Do they all line up with God's Word? Is the content healthy? Is it facilitating a closer walk with God? Is it pulling you down? Is your heart still hopeful? Don't take this for granted and assume everything is okay. Rather, ask God to shine the torchlight of His Spirit to illuminate your mind so you can see what is *really* going on.

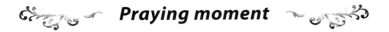 *Praying moment*

Based on what has been shared in the previous section on the mind, take the time to bring your observations and concerns in the form of a prayer. Tell God about the specific changes you would like to see and enlist the Holy Spirit to help you on your journey.

Confront your fears ... deal with the 'what ifs'

> 'For God has not given us a spirit of fear and timidity, but of power, love, and self-discipline.'
> (*2 Timothy 1:7, NLT*)

Have you ever considered what life would be like if you never got the very thing you wanted? Many of us don't even broach this thought because, after all, God will answer our cry, come through for us and meet our every need. And we have a 101 scriptures to back this up.

But what if ... ?

Could you live with the fact that you don't get what you desire? What if it was Gods desire for you to remain as you are – be it for a season or for the rest of your life? Could you face God again? Could you lay the issue to rest and get on with your life? Tough questions, I know, but we still have to confront our fears. After all, it is *our fear* of not getting what we want that perturbs many of us to the point of discouragement and depression. We become troubled as we ponder secretly on the possibility of our not getting the outcome we want. Could Rachael live with the fact that she may never have a child? I am not saying that is the case but – what if? Could Lola accept the fact she may remain single? Both these ladies had normal desires, as did Jason in wanting a job to provide for his family and Richard who wanted to serve God. Yet, I am confident that God has a plan for all four of them as He has for you and me. As for the details of the plan, that is left to be seen. But it will unfold over the course of time. We just have to keep hoping and believing.

When we fail to acknowledge the 'what if', our fears start to eat us up inside. In our helplessness, we begin to get anxious. This alone can trigger discouragement. Thoughts like, 'What if He does not come through?' plague our mind and send us into a state of panic. And, because we don't like dealing with such unnerving feelings, we ditch such thoughts and try to whip ourselves up with scriptures.

Confronting our fears and/or dealing with the 'what if' scenarios of our lives is not about giving up hope or ceasing to trust God. I believe God can do anything! He can make our friend Rachael a mother, even in her menopausal years. He can promote Jason with a job offer as a company director or even give him a business of his own. Lola can find a guy, even when she is not looking and Richard could end up being the next Billy Graham. But for now, to them, it seems as if their prayers are not working or that God has abandoned them. But we all know that is not the case.

This is not about giving up but simply learning to enter God's rest. By placing our desires in God's hands we eliminate our stress, fear and anxiety. It is really about hoping till the very end, regardless of what happens. This, in itself, takes real courage because you are relinquishing control to Someone else's hands, trusting that they will deliver on what they say.

Dealing with our 'what ifs' forces us to look beyond our present and consider the bigger picture God might have in mind. It compels us to contemplate what God might want to accomplish during this season of our lives. It makes us ponder on the 101 other ways God could be glorified in our lives. Moreover, we get the opportunity to reflect on our relationship with God and the basis upon which it is built (e.g. seeking His hand and not His face). A good indication of a reluctance to place ourselves in His hands could be if we have a tendency of drawing away from Him when we don't get our way. Can we be relied on to keep marching ahead, regardless of what we do or don't get from Him?

Confronting our fears also affords us the opportunity to be at peace with ourselves. I don't know about you, but I find that carrying such a weight can be burdensome. But, by handing them over to Him we no longer have to worry about how something will be done. All we have to do is trust and obey – like the old hymn says.

This still remains a challenge for many of us. Personally, it was a tough one for me to grasp and I could not bear the thought of not getting what I desired. After all, I had prayed about it, right? Earlier, I mentioned two particular cases where I had prayed that a person I knew, who had a life-threatening illness, would pull through. Well, both of them died and I often wonder if I could have prepared myself better or recovered quicker from the ordeal had I stood back to consider what Father might have wanted to do in each situation. Of course, we only had one outcome in mind – that they both survive the ordeal. Perhaps there were other possibilities we couldn't anticipate and, having done our best, we just needed to rest in God's sovereignty. I feel that, when we start to consider possible alternatives, it may come across as lacking faith. This may be the case but the only way we can judge this is to look at our motives and what's going on within us.

Another scenario where God demonstrated He had other plans was at the crucifixion of Jesus. To Jesus' disciples and followers, all hope would have seemed lost as He took His last breath on the cross. To them, it was finished, a closed case. But God still had a plan which we see later unfold. And if all the churches of that time observed a time of fasting and prayer against Jesus being crucified, such a prayer would never have been answered. Why? Because it went against God's greater plan for the salvation of humanity. That was far more important to Him than anything else – even His Son.

It all comes back to whether we trust God to make the right decisions for our lives. Because if we don't, discouragement may find its way into our hearts.

Lastly, regarding the point about God not sparing His

only Son from the cross so that He could achieve His plans, it may be worth considering whether we, who claim to walk in the footsteps of Jesus, truly allow ourselves to be God's suffering servants, prepared to experience hardship for the greater good. It is worth considering.

Enlightening moment

'Rest in the LORD, and wait patiently for Him;
Do not fret because of him who prospers in his way ...'
(*Psalm 37:7, NKJ*)

'Let be and be still, and know (recognize and understand)
that I am God.
I will be exalted among the nations! I will be
exalted in the earth.'
(*Psalm 46:10, AMP*)

Discover what has changed

'I don't know about you, but I'm running hard for the finish line. I'm giving it everything I've got. No sloppy living for me! I'm staying alert and in top condition ...'
(*1 Corinthians 9:26-27, MSG*)

Now your immediate thoughts may go to your unmet need or unresolved issue. It could be that this has been longstanding matter or maybe the situation has risen recently. Either way, it is here and real. If you asked Rachael, she would point to her failed fertility treatment, and quite rightly so. Jason would point to his joblessness which was making him feel hopeless. Lola had her heart broken time after time and Richard hopes of becoming a pastor were ebbing away. These are real life situations that can rock the foundations of our worlds, much less our faith. They stare at us glaringly in the face. We are confronted with them awake and they continue to trouble us in our sleep.

So, like these four individuals, you may quickly conclude that your experiences with discouragement all boil down to the challenge(s) you are facing. And this could indeed be the case as I don't want to deny the fact that our earthly plights can be trying. However, I want to encourage you to put this aside for a moment.

Life checkpoints

Over the years, I have noticed that there can be other contributory factors that might result in us feeling frustrated, troubled and discouraged – not just the particular difficulty we are facing. One such factor is change. These are the changes we experience in our world that bring us out of balance with ourselves and can have an impact on us. Whilst change is inevitable, we have to manage it by first becoming aware of its existence and then taking action to realign ourselves. Overlooking a change or even denying its existence does not help. Rather, it is important to identify and acknowledge that something somewhere has changed.

To help you dig deeper, I will briefly touch on some areas in our lives where change can occur. I encourage you to reflect on these and see how they might relate to you.

Relationships

Relationships are important and can have an impact on how we feel, think and behave. For instance, if we pull away from others or they withdraw from us, we can start to feel isolated and lonely. And there is a link between isolation/loneliness and discouragement. I believe this is why God demonstrates effective relationship models from the beginning of creation. First, we have the Godhead existing as Father, Son and Holy Spirit. Then God went on to create the males and females of all species. Then He instituted the concept of marriage and family. Whilst on earth, Jesus was in constant communion with the Father. And so we see the concept of relationship modelled throughout the Bible, giving us a strong indication of how important it is.

Although we know relationships are important, it isn't just a case of having anyone around. (After all, you can be surrounded by a multitude and still be isolated.) Rather, it is about having supportive people who can demonstrate the love and grace of God in your life and with whom you can reciprocate. The last thing you want around you are unsupportive, abusive, negative, overbearing, discouraging, dream-killing or hurtful people. Surrounding yourself with people like that will only adversely affect you. Looking back on Rachael's case, if she were to have the full support of her husband, standing up for her when her in-laws showed up and giving her emotional support when she needed it, she would be able to stand her failed fertility treatment and be hopeful of the next round.

With this in mind, you may want to reassess the quality of your relationships as well as any changes that might have occurred.

Questions to ask yourself:

- how would you describe your relationship with others (e.g. family, friends, peers, pastor, boss)?

- have you experienced any loss or breakdown of key relationships (past or present) that could be affecting you (e.g. divorce, bereavement, relocation)?

- are you feeling isolated or lonely as a result of your withdrawing from others or others withdrawing from you?

- would you say you have supportive people around you?

- are there presently any relationships you need to break off or rebuild?

Personal and regular routines

Having a regular routine of prayer, studying of scripture, attending church, and other spiritual activities and practices has been shown to benefit ones mental health, according to the Royal College of Psychiatrists, and can help in times of distress, emotional stress, physical illness, loss, and bereavement.

I have noticed that a small shift in my routine can have a huge and sometimes detrimental impact on how I feel. Take, for example, when I have had a really busy week travelling and, as a result, 'cut corners' on my quiet time. If I fail to redress the imbalance quickly, by the end of the week I start to feel guilty, ashamed and down. Years back, I would have felt so condemned that I could not enjoy the worship experience in church because I felt like a hypocrite. The devil certainly had a field day, reminding me of how inadequate I was as a Christian. Thank God He intercepted those thoughts and set me free from the feeling of condemnation (*Romans 8:1*). As a loving Father, He encouraged me to get back on track rather than continue down the slippery slope I was on called 'discouragement'.

But here is the important point: during those seasons when I let my regular quiet times slip, I also had challenging issues I was facing. I could have concluded that my feelings of discouragement were entirely due to those challenging issues when, in fact, the actual culprit was the break in my regular quiet time routine. These everyday moments uplift me and gave me the fortitude to keep going. Without them, discouragement has a tendency of knocking on my door.

It is not just our routines around our spiritual needs that are important. Other routines are valuable to maintain too: those around rest, sleep, eating well, and much more. I also notice that, every so often, I need to inject an element of fun – whether it is listening or dancing to music, enjoying nature, or swimming – or else I can get grouchy when life just seems to be all work and no play. The only way I can describe it is like being on a diet for life with no opportunity to have a chocolate cookie or bar of chocolate. Where's the fun? Again, if I don't carefully assess the situation – why I'm feeling discouraged – I may put the blame on something else ... including God, who called me to serve Him.

Questions to ask yourself:

- what daily routines do you have in place?

    o spiritual routines, e.g. prayer/quiet times, studying of scripture, attending church, etc.

    o physical/social routines, e.g. sleep, rest, eating/drinking, recreation, meeting friends, playing in a team, etc.

- are these routines adequate to help you live an abundant life? If not, what changes can you make today?

Lifestyle changes

Life-changing situations can affect all of us. Those major changes in our personal circumstances, such as marriage, divorce, having a child, taking on a big project, a promotion, relocation, illness, bereavement or redundancy, tend to have a big impact on us, especially if we are not adequately prepared for change or have underestimated what the change would translate to in reality. There are some changes, such as bereavement, that life can never adequately prepare you for but even if a change is considered a positive one, such as marriage, childbirth or promotion, it can still be very unsettling. My point is that when we are looking at why we may be feeling discouraged, we need to take into account all those things that might be going on in the background of our lives, both negative and positive.

Let's take an example: you are given a promotion with a huge pay increase along with a lot of perks. However, it means relocating away from family and friends which may make you feel isolated and lonely. Moreover, you now have a huge role with loads of responsibility and they're expecting you to hit the ground running. Whilst you have been a high achiever in your previous position, you quickly discover that you need to acquire new skills, attitudes and behaviours to help you succeed. In addition to this, you are now working with a different group of people who have their own values, culture and way of working. After the first week, you start to wonder if this was the right move for you. It is easy to see how you may start to feel out of your depth, pressured, anxious and isolated. These feelings are all classic contributors to a troubled soul and a discouraged heart.

By the way, it's worth noting that our reactions to change (such as the promotion scenario I mentioned) should not be interpreted as an indication of weakness (though I am sure it may be the case for some). I believe we all have strengths and areas in need of development (i.e. weaknesses) that can work for or against us during change. However, I also believe that the key thing is to maximise our strengths and get help filling the gaps. First, we need to acknowledge change (seeing that it is inevitable), then make the necessary steps to help us with the transition. Remember how Jason, who had been jobless for eighteen months, had become discouraged after a while, although he did not start that way. He did all the right things – like remaining hopeful, studying scripture, praying, etc. – but he did have gaps, the main one being his not having the right people around him to keep him encouraged throughout this period of transition in his life. His hands simply got tired and, unlike Moses, he did not have an Aaron and Hur to hold them up for him.

A question to ask yourself:

Have there been any major lifestyle changes (e.g. working longer hours, taking on a big project, increased roles/responsibilities, a promotion, getting married, having a child, change of location etc.) that could be affecting you in more ways than you might have acknowledged?

Unresolved or unfinished issues

These issues can stem from our childhood or adulthood. They can end up causing problems in differing areas of our lives because we have chosen not to deal with them or don't know how to. In my previous book, *Overcoming Emotional Baggage: A Woman's Guide to Living the Abundant Life*, I talk about the significance this emotional baggage can have on us. Simply put, I believe that it hinders us from growing, spiritually and emotionally. Emotional baggage has been the culprit in many perturbed and disheartened individuals' lives. And yet, when we don't see the links in our lives, we can completely misdiagnose what's really going on and blame other things.

Earlier, we considered the story of Lola, the high flying business woman who was unhappily single at forty-five. She had become discouraged after her latest episode with Steve and had decided to give up on the matter of marriage altogether. However, this was not the first time Lola had been abandoned – other men had done the same to her in the past. The fact was that she had underlying issues with rejection and lack of trust and she approached every potential relationship with this lurking about in the background. It was something that had occurred over the course of time but the result was that not only did she decide to ditch the idea of finding Mr Right but also her trust in God to bring it to pass.

The good news is that, with God's help, we can get rid of our baggage and be made whole. By the way, being made whole has nothing to do with getting what we want. For instance, Lola's breaking from the negatives of her past – her restoration – will not be dependent on her getting married or not. I mention this because we tend to think we can only feel better when we get what we want. This way of thinking is a mistake – we can be alleviated from our discouraged hearts and troubled souls whilst still trusting God to bring us what we seek.

Questions to ask yourself:

- are there one or more unresolved or unfinished issues in your life that may be the cause of your discouraged heart and troubled soul?

- could these be camouflaged by your current needs or situation?

Stress and burnout

Being under constant stress can lead to one feeling depressed. If you are trying to keep all your balls in the air in a serious juggling act, and you have too many pressures, demanding too much of you physically and mentally – then you could be leading to burnout. When under stress, you tend to feel that if you could just finish this one last task or stay up just one more night, you are making progress. And when you reach burnout you find yourself in a place where everything, all feeling, has been used up by prolonged and excessive stress. You have lost your motivation and feel powerless, exhausted, frustrated, apathetic, lethargic, and hopeless.

It could be that stress or burnout may be the culprit behind how you are feeling. So it helps to take a moment to consider what might be going on in your world.

Questions to ask yourself:

- are you under pressure in any area of your life (e.g. work, home, church, or relationships)?

- do you feel pressured to perform, conform, and live up to others expectations?

- do you feel like you are constantly having to juggle several balls?

- when was the last time you had a break – and I mean a real break?

- reflect back on your life and consider if there is a chance you could be suffering from burnout?

You might be wondering what all this has to do with your discouraged heart? It has *everything* to do with it. Many times, we forget that we are tripartite beings made up of spirit, soul and body. These three are intricately intertwined and whatever you do (or don't do) to one affects the others. There is no way, for instance, that you can deplete your spirit and not expect your soul to be affected. And a troubled soul will eventually affect your physical wellbeing (this has been scientifically proven – leaving the medical field baffled by a number of 'modern' syndromes and diseases). The same goes for your physical body – treat it carelessly for long enough (or push it too hard) and it will affect your spirit, mind, and emotions. Get the point?

Our problem arises when we try to deal with our spirit, soul and body in isolation. To avoid this, we need to take a step back and think holistically – just as the medical field is now being forced to do. For us, this means taking a closer look at what might be bringing discouragement into our hearts. Is it solely due to our pressing needs or the waiting for answers to our prayers? Is there a change in your life or other contributory factor that could be propagating discouragement? In which case, could your perceived need simply be a smokescreen? Only you can answer this by probing further. When you do, you may uncover the fact that you have other contributory factors than simply the need your mind has been focused on. Either way, you are now in a better place to manage your situation and take action to bring about your inner peace.

 *Journaling moment*

We have spent some time considering changes in our lives that can promote discouragement. So why not take some time out to identify any areas of your life that may have changed and brought you out of sync. Bring them before God in prayer. After this, your next step is to take specific action to help you move forward. For example: if you have found yourself drifting away from people, take an action that could reconnect you (e.g. visit a friend, invite someone to your home, call someone); or if your quiet time seems to have dwindled, free up some time in your day to increase it (e.g. spend less time watching TV – even if it is Christian TV!; reduce/cut out time on the internet or phone; maximise your lunch breaks at work; wake up earlier/sleep later, etc.) Remember, your personal time with God is paramount.

Check your heart

'Create in me a clean heart, O God ...'
(*Psalm 51:10, NLT*)

We touched briefly on this when we were exploring our daily routines and I would like to expand somewhat on it. It is one thing to have our daily practices in place but it is another to be able to assess objectively the true state of our hearts.

In our journey through life, we can pick up spiritual baggage, just as we do with emotional baggage, and we need to discern when we might have amassed any. This identifying process in itself can be a challenge for us, and it can be harder still to work out the possible impact such spiritual baggage could have our inner wellbeing. More often than not, we are quick to attribute any inner turmoil to other factors, such as our unmet needs.

If you were to go to your doctor and complain about feeling down (and other symptoms) there is a chance you may be wrongly diagnosed with depression. Suffering from the effects of unresolved spiritual issues will trigger some of the same symptoms, such as feelings of dejection, guilt, hopelessness, helplessness, an inability to concentrate, insomnia, change in appetite, or thoughts of death.

Take, for example, an unconfessed sin that is eating a person up inside. This could trigger depression-like symptoms along with feelings of shame. In such a scenario, the individual would benefit from godly counselling and guidance to help bring the issue to light. Part of the journey will require them bringing the matter (i.e. the sin) before God and receiving His forgiveness, grace, and mercy. Using the Bible, they would need to be reassured of their standing with God and His love towards them. Through this process, the individual would be realigned with God and brought back in fellowship with Him. As a follow up, they can be encouraged to grow spiritually and strengthen their relationship with God through the likes of prayer, joining a Bible study group, being discipled for accountability and support. Of course, the steps taken will depend on the nature of the issue or sin. With the weight of the sin off their shoulders, I believe they will, over time, feel alleviated of their original symptoms of a discouraged heart and a troubled soul.

We need to become more perceptive and attentive to what is going on spiritually. And there is value in having people in our lives who can be our 'eyes' and 'ears' – especially if we are liable to lose sight of our realities. If you cast your mind back to the story of David, you will remember that Prophet Nathan was David's eyes, ears and conscience when he committed adultery with Bathsheba (*2 Samuel 12*). David became sorrowful after his sin was exposed and confessed, hence we have *Psalm 51*. Peter, too, wept bitterly and felt guilty for denying Jesus Christ (*Luke 22: 54–65*).

Therefore, during times of discouragement, we can't rule out unresolved spiritual matters as a contributing factor.

Journaling moment

Now, I would like you to consider the following questions about aspects of your spiritual life, with the aim of uncovering potential causes of your discouraged heart and troubled soul:

- **have my spiritual reservoirs become depleted as a result of my journey in life?** A classic example was Elijah who was exhausted on many levels and needed to recuperate after his huge feat on Mount Carmel (*1 Kings 19*). Could it be that at this time, just like Elijah, your focus ought to be on your recovery strategy (such as taking a retreat or vacation, eating well, resting, etc.). Without this, you could be setting yourself up for failure or a fall. Trust me, none of us is superhuman and if God could take time out to rest after the Creation, so can you

- **has my present need or situation become so challenging and exhausting that I need the help of others to get me through it?** When the necessary support is not there, it can have adverse consequences. This happened to Moses whose hands got tired when Joshua and his men were fighting the Amalekites. As a result, when his hand, which was holding the staff of God, came down, their enemies got the upper hand. To maintain a victorious stance, he needed Aaron and Hur to support him by seating him on a stone and holding up his arms (*Exodus 17:8–13*). So, in your case, maybe you need support. Do you have people around you who could support you through your situation(s)? We all need our very own 'Aaron and Hur' in our lives or else we will struggle

- **could my disobedience to God be troubling me?** There are times when God wants us to go one way but we decide to go another. When we do this, we never find peace until we find our way back to God. Jonah experienced this, hence his prayer in *Jonah 2*. The prodigal son recognised the error of his ways and decided to come back home to his loving father. So do you need to find your way back to God? If so, what changes do you need to make? If you have been disobeying God's spiritual principles – such as forgiveness, dealing with anger, being unjust, etc. – it needs to be dealt with so they do not become a stumbling block in your relationship with God and others. Again, this needs careful consideration as well as God's help to enlighten our understanding as some of these may be buried deep within us or may go way back into our past

- **am I feeling burdened or concerned about a matter in my heart?** This could be to do with your own life or it could extend beyond, as it was with Nehemiah who was concerned about the news he heard about Jerusalem (*Nehemiah 1*). It was noted that he sat down and wept and then mourned, fasted, and prayed for many days. Daniel's visions also troubled him (*Daniel 7:28*). At times, certain issues trouble us but we struggle to see the link with how we are feeling. A busy and cluttered lifestyle can dull our senses and deprive us of carving out adequate time to seek God when we can consult Him on what action we should take. One thing is for sure: ignoring such feelings is not the answer and we need to adopt Nehemiah's and Daniel's approach which was to get God involved

- **have I been faced with one or more personal setbacks that have made me feel down in the dumps?** The fact is we all get down sometimes when personal setbacks or tragedies occur. By their very nature, they have a tendency to weigh us down – just ask Job (*Job 10*) and Asaph (*Psalm 73*). Regardless of how spiritual or 'strong' you feel you may be, you may find yourself feeling discouraged. However, like David, you need to strengthen yourself in the Lord and wait patiently for God to act on your behalf (*Psalm 37:7*). We have to learn to leave it in His hands and trust He will come through for us

- **have I lost hope? Do I still trust God?** Our hope is the anchor that keeps us steadfast in a tumultuous storm (*Hebrews 6:18–20*). However, when hope dwindles it affects our outlook which in turn affects our moods and feelings. We get tossed back and forth by the winds of our circumstances. We feel helpless and unable to do anything about it. In such times, we lose sight of the greatness of God and focus entirely on the situation. Without building up our trust again in God (e.g. reading the Bible, praying, having uplifting people around us, etc.), we may find ourselves drifting into the ranks of those who feel they have nothing to live for or who feel life is hopeless. However, because we have an eternal assurance, we now need to refocus our minds on the awesomeness of God. This can be done in a number of ways: placing ourselves in an uplifting atmosphere (e.g. church, study groups); reading/listening to the Bible and resources to build up our hopes again; and sharing our hopes and fears with others.

DIGGING DEEPER BEYOND YOUR UNMET NEED

PART 4

STRENGTH FOR THE JOURNEY

Chapter 7

Journeying into our tomorrows

'Wait and hope for an expect the Lord; be brave and of good courage and let your heart be stout and enduring. Yes, wait for and hope for and expect the Lord.'
(*Psalm 27:14, AMP*)

Strength for today, hope for tomorrow

Richard's journey continued

'God is not man, one given to lies, and not a son of man changing his mind.
Does he speak and not do what he says? Does he promise and not come through?'
(*Numbers 23:19, MSG*)

After a period of going off-course, Richard decided it was time to confide in his mentor, Tom, about the feelings and concerns he had about his calling. During his first meeting with Tom, Richard broke down and wept – something that took him by surprise. He mourned the lost years and deferred dreams. His mentor, who was able to empathise as he had had a similar experience in his earlier years in ministry, provided him with guidance and support. His first suggestion was for Richard to relinquish his current roles and responsibilities in church and focus on redressing his relationship with God. Part of the process was to include a time of solitude in a retreat. As for the initial step, he suggested Richard repent of his negative attitudes and behaviours. One clear message Tom delivered was that it was clear that Richard needed God's help to navigate through his current wilderness experience. Rather than leaving God out or resenting Him, Tom suggested he invite Him into the situation, as the solution to the matter rested in God's hands.

Richard found this challenging at first, the reason being that he had blamed God for his predicament. But with the encouragement of Tom, Richard took small yet deliberate steps that included prayer and studying of the Word. The aim was to rekindle the flames of his once raging heart. Tom checked in on him regularly. This allowed Richard to share his thoughts, hopes and challenges whilst Tom's wisdom and experience – coupled with maturity in faith – provided a forum for Richard to take strides in overcoming his discouraged heart and troubled soul. Richard started to see the changes in himself as he made himself accountable to Tom. He was grateful to have someone there who took an interest in his Christian growth and calling.

Over time, Richard was able to open up to God and share his disappointments. He found being truthful with God, as Tom had suggested, was a turning point in his journey. With the heaviness lifted from him, his outlook changed. He felt a renewed hope – something he had not felt for a long time. Whilst he still did not have a ministry, deep within himself he began to feel hopeful that God had a plan. What sparked this off was a conversation Tom had with him, encouraging him to speak to God about His plans for him. Though the years of silence had sown seeds of doubt in Richard's mind, Tom reminded him of the fact that God always has a plan. And by remaining close to God, God will reveal His purpose and order his steps.

As Richard spent more time with God, he became more confident than ever that God was indeed preparing him for greatness. And, when Richard parted ways with Tom after an uplifting few months, Tom's parting words would often be replayed in his mind: 'Be sure of the fact that if your call is of God, no man can hold you back. In time, God will unfold his plans. So hold on to what God has told you.' With this, Richard felt an inner assurance that everything would be okay.

This is a message for all of us who are holding on to our God-given visions and dreams. No matter what our present realities look like, God's plans for our lives stand. So even when it seems like our dreams are fading away, we must hold on, in faith, trusting that God is in control. Do not let your present circumstances cloud your understanding of who God is and how His abilities can turn your situation around. Better still: find others who can hold up your dream even when you are struggling to do so, like Richard did. Stay away from dream killers who may suggest you relinquish what God has called you to do. Every so often, check in with the Dream-giver (God) for assurance, and to prevent any seeds of doubt, anxiety, fear or discouragement being sown. And if the dream, goal or purpose is from Him, the facts of your present realities simply don't count.

Nothing Is Impossible

Lola's journey continued

> 'For nothing is impossible with God.'
> (*Luke 1:37, NLT*)

Lola was taken aback by her pastor's question: 'If God can do all that He has done in your life thus far, can

He not bring the right man along? Is anything too hard for the Lord?' He had noticed that she had been away from church for a while and whenever he had tried to reach her, she was always too busy to talk. So, weeks later, he had been delighted to see her in church one Sunday morning and had asked her to stay behind for a quick chat.

Shortly into their chat, it came to light that Lola had broken up with Steve and that the experience had troubled her. She explained that, as a result, she had concluded that she could no longer trust God on the matter any more. Rather than keep getting hurt, she would focus on her work and take it that she was meant to be single all her life.

But the pastor's question intrigued her. 'Is anything too hard for the Lord?'. She had spent weeks trying to push the whole 'Steve' saga to the back of her mind, though deep down she knew she had only buried the hurt and pain. She did not know where her faith was right now because it seemed that God had let her down. After all, she had prayed and fasted. All her hopes had been pinned on Steve but those, along with her faith, had been dashed. Now, her strategy was to stay away from God, at least till she got her mind clear on things.

However, each time Lola picked up her Bible, it seemed to fall on the same page. She did not take any notice at first until the third, fourth and fifth time it happened. Time after time, her Bible fell open on *Genesis 18:14* which asked the very same question her pastor had just asked her. Was God trying to tell her something? She had to conclude that God was indeed trying to put a point across.

On returning home that night, Lola did something she had not done in a while. She got on her knees and prayed. Using the same scripture, she asked herself, 'Was anything too difficult for God?'. After all, here she was, the envy of most people – an accomplished business woman and philanthropist who was known worldwide. By His grace, she had accomplished in only a few years what many never see in their lifetime. She had all the money and comfort she needed. Moreover, she had been able to share her time and money building other people's lives too. 'So could the same God not bring me my Boaz? Can my God not find me my Isaac?', she said to herself.

By the time Lola had finished praying, she had repented for her attitudes, for shutting God out and completely overlooking all He had done for her. Maybe all her experiences had amounted to God trying to preserve her for the one He was preparing for her. Maybe all her own efforts to find a husband were actually scuppering God's intentions. As she prayed, Lola became convinced that God 'was going to make a way where there seemed to be no way', as the scripture said. She decided to get on with business as usual and focus on her work, only this time things would be different: This time, her actions would be fuelled by her newfound assurance – that there is nothing God cannot do.

If you have ever found yourself in Lola's situation, waiting for God to intervene in a matter that concerns you, I encourage you to ponder on the scripture, mentioned above, that says:

> 'Is anything too hard for the LORD?'
> (*Genesis 18:14, NKJ*)

Is your situation really too difficult for God? Is the matter so weighty that even He can't accomplish it? Really? If those are our thoughts, then our first step must be to refocus our perspective. Though the situation may seem like an insurmountable mountain to us, the God we serve is much greater than that. He is the Rock higher than any other rock. Nothing compares to Him.

In addition to this truth, Lola learnt another valuable

lesson. She recognised that while she did not have this particular thing she wanted, God had blessed her with other things. Could the same be said about you? Maybe you are doing well in your career or business? Maybe you have good health? Maybe God has placed roles or responsibilities in your hands? Maybe you have food to eat and a house over your head? Maybe you have been blessed with a great family or friends? Better still, you've been blessed with the fact that God loves you – you are saved and know that Heaven awaits you.

One conviction I have is that as God puts His plan in place. He never leaves us comfortless. He comforts us with other things almost as if to say, 'Child, I am working on your case. However, in the meantime, have this as a sign that I will make good My Word.' This is not like His giving us a pacifier, as we do to babies to stop them from crying (though this may be the case for some of us), but, rather, to keep us ever aware of the fact that He can do more than we even ask or think of. His gifts remind us of the fact that He has not forgotten us, that our names are written on the palms of His hands. It is done to keep us in a hopeful state.

Using a biblical example, the same God who brought the children of Israel through the Red Sea could be relied upon to help them drive out the inhabitants of the Promised Land. Moreover, if you remember, not only did He provide them with manna to eat daily but He preserved the clothes on their backs and the sandals on their feet for forty years. Now if that is not a sign to show He remains committed, I don't know what else could be.

When we focus dogmatically on what we lack, we completely miss the daily miracles, signs and wonders He performs. In the past, I have fallen into this trap and sometimes it takes more than these wondrous daily acts that I make a note of in my prayer journal to jerk the slack out of me. Sometimes, God uses other methods to remind me of this fact. He has used my mum (bless her) on a number of occasions to remind me of my miracles as I journeyed through my personal wilderness. Also, He leads me to certain stories in the Bible that confront me with my own oversight and disbelief. When I become enlightened, I fall on my knees, like Lola, and ask for forgiveness. I also ask for strength because my discouraged heart and troubled soul are a symptom of the fatigue I feel as a result of my journey in my wilderness. Time has a way of wearing us down but God has a way of giving us a new wind beneath our wings so that we can soar even higher than before, regardless of the outcome.

Weeping may last for the night ...

Rachael's journey continued

> 'The nights of crying your eyes out give way to days of laughter.'
> (*Psalm 30:5, NLT*)

From the moment Rachael picked herself from the bathroom floor, she just knew her days of weeping were coming to an end. Although she did not have a newsflash from Heaven nor did an angel appear to her, yet somehow, deep within her, she knew. OK, a lot of money had been spent on the fertility treatment but she was willing to trust God again. This battle was certainly not over.

Rachael decided to stop blaming herself with the things she did or did not do. She also decided to stop blaming God. Instead, she would pick up where she left off, continuing to keep praying in faith. This time, her attitude was going to be different.

Daniel, her husband, could hardly comprehend the difference in Rachael. Normally, after she had lost a baby, he would expect her to cry for weeks. Instead, she acted normally, almost as if nothing had happened. Then he noticed that she was getting up earlier these days and would be found downstairs, on her face, praying. She printed out scriptures pertaining to giving birth and plastered them all over the house – on the fridge door and bathroom mirror. She would spend hours worshipping God, sometimes, all through the night. As far as she was concerned, she was going to remain in His presence – no matter what – baby or not. Of course, her desire was to give birth someday, but she decided she did not want it to be the centre or the sole focus of her life or marriage. She was done being discouraged. Fifteen years was long enough. She wanted her life back.

She also wanted her marriage back. She and Daniel seemed estranged these days and, with Gods help, Rachael was determined to make things work with him. After all, although Daniel wanted children, it was not the end of the world to him if it didn't happen. Rachael realised that she had made it so. Now that she knew that she had been pushing Daniel away she knew that she needed the wisdom of God to help her. There were times when Daniel had tried to comfort her in the past but all she had done was reject his love and comfort. As for her in-laws, she needed wisdom and strength to deal with them. Rachael realised that the whole matter needed God's intervention. And, rather than carrying on weeping, she was going to 'fix up' and get on with life.

In Rachael's case, we see a sudden turnaround. I believe that when God relieves us from the spirit of discouragement, we start to see a dramatic change in our attitudes, beliefs and behaviours. We expect this to be our reaction when our prayers are answered and we get what we want. However, Rachael's case proves to us that we can still remain hopeful and maintain our stance, even through the storms. A classic example of this was when Paul and Silas worshipped God in the midnight whilst in prison (*Acts 16*). In times like this, we demonstrate the faith we claim to have. That is not to say we will be euphoric during stormy times, but our actions are the ones that determine our beliefs. Our actions demonstrate that we have the hope and faith we say we have. And we can still lift up holy hands and heartily pray to and worship God with tears streaming down our faces. The tears are not a sign of weakness, more a sign of our humanity and an expression of our emotions to God.

The question is whether we too can be found rejoicing in the midst of the storm. Can we keep pressing on despite our setbacks? It can be tough sometimes but it is about digging deep within us so we too can encourage ourselves in the Lord (*1 Samuel 30:1–6*).

Rachael had decided to serve God regardless of whether she got what she wanted, although her desire still remained. And so, when we too can confidently say to God, 'It does not matter anymore' or 'Let Your will be done regardless of my desires' you will know that you have truly placed your life in His capable hands, serving Him faithfully, even if your wishes haven't been fulfilled.

God can do it without me

Jason's journey continued

'It is not by force nor by strength, but by my Spirit, says the Lord of Heaven's Armies.'
(*Zechariah 4:6, NLT*)

Jason had done everything conceivable to get a job: he had registered with umpteen agencies; he had had his CV professionally written; he had registered with untold online job websites making his profile available globally; he scoured newspapers daily; and was applying for an average of thirty jobs a week. He was on the internet day and night applying for this one, tweaking his CV or covering letter for that one. But the result was still the same – nothing. In short, he did everything he could and now he was getting desperate.

It is no surprise that we see Jason becoming discouraged, especially as he had backed up his efforts with prayer, although this eventually dwindled as did his hope. However, it was the last letter of rejection that did it. It crushed him. It was the straw that broke the camel's back. He was banking on getting this job, especially after making it to the final rounds of interviews. 'What's the point of putting so much effort into something when nothing comes of it?' he thought. 'What is the point?'

To make matters worse, Jason noticed how shabby Lisa's clothes were looking. She used to be in the latest fashion lines but was now having to go to second-hand charity shops to buy what she needed because she had sold anything of value to help make ends meet. His kids were outgrowing their clothes and shoes and he had been hoping the new job could help with these. Christmas was coming and he wanted to put a smile on their faces. 'Wasn't I supposed to be the provider?' was the thought that plagued his mind. Little by little he sunk lower and lower into the mire of discouragement. It was as if God wasn't paying attention to all his efforts. Was he supposed to keep looking for a job? Should he intensify his actions? Did God want him to start his own business like someone suggested? 'What should I do?' he thought.

Lisa noticed Jason had become distant and withdrawn and she had the idea of asking one of his good friends, Jonathan, to speak to him. Jonathan ended up being a great help and source of encouragement. In their chats in the nearby pub, Jason finally had the opportunity to share his fears and concerns with a trusted friend. During their conversation, he mentioned that he felt like he was a failure — all his efforts seemed to yield nothing. He went on to share how much effort he had put in over the past eighteen months, and how it seemed that God was not helping matters.

Jonathan, on hearing his friend's troubles, asked Jason whether he had considered taking a break from the job search. At first, it seemed to Jason an absurd idea — after all, how were potential employers to find him? However, Jonathan pointed out that, although Jason had invested a lot of energy in finding a job, perhaps he had not given God room to manoeuvre in the situation. It seemed to him that Jason's efforts were all based on trying to make things happen with his own strength as opposed to having complete reliance on God. Although he was doing the right things, his fears had formed the base of it all, rather than his faith. It was as if he had been saying to God, 'It's all right, I've got this one covered'. And now, he had run himself ragged and run out of steam.

Jonathan shared from his past experience. 'At times,' he said, 'faith is all about standing still even when everything within you, or even others, are compelling you to do otherwise.' He mentioned that, during a time of personal crisis of his own, he had found comfort in *Psalm 37:7* that said:

'Rest in the LORD, and wait patiently for Him;
Do not fret because of him who prospers in his way ...'
(*NKJ*)

Jonathan had realised that the trick was to rest in God and simply wait for Him to act on his behalf. Though this was hard at first, when he did do it, he experienced a deep sense of peace. And, sure enough, God came through in the end. Moreover, the solution came through by no effort of his own. God came through.

Jonathan asked Jason to consider stepping back from the situation, giving himself a breather whilst getting back in line with God. His time out could be beneficial in seeking God's face on the matter and ask for direction for this season or perhaps the next one in his life.
With a bit of persuasion, Jason agreed to this strange 'hands off' approach till at least he could see the wood for the trees. Jonathan mentioned that he had seen an

advert in the paper where a local charity was looking for a volunteer to help with some project they were running in the local community centre. Jason decided to go along to take his mind off things. Although he thought the job was beneath him he went anyway. From the moment he arrived at the centre, he felt God was up to something. He warmed to the project manager and, before he knew it, he had got stuck in. Although it was a voluntary role, for the first time in a very long time he felt a sense of peace. The fear, anxiety and discouragement that had been hanging over his head had gone. It seemed that the break had been exactly what he needed while he was trying to figure things out.

In the first week, Jason fought hard not apply for jobs. By the second week, though, he finally decided to let go and let God. He notified staff at his local job centre of his volunteer role. He planned to resume job hunting, in the near future – if that was what he felt God wanted him to do. In the meantime, he planned to hand over the reins of job hunting to God. For now, his real job was to stop fretting and learn to trust Him.

As you can see, it appears that our four individuals have managed to get on with their lives with the support of God and others. Whilst they have not received what they hoped for, we can see a move towards spiritual maturity and growth. We see a new ray of hope and a deeper reliance on their faith in God. From the pit of discouragement, we see them gradually move towards a place called 'encouraged'. They are now gravitating, by faith, to the spot of light at the end of the tunnel. But note: this migration is a journey. Some take longer than others but they get there through a change in attitudes, beliefs and behaviours. With others there to support them and a determination on their part, they will see the light become bigger and bigger as they draw closer.

Will they all get what they want? Time and God alone can tell. But I am hoping that you see how this book isn't really about becoming encouraged through getting our needs met. It is much more than that. It is about maintaining our faith and holding on (by any means possible, I might add) until the very end of our life's journey. It is about developing our faith in God and growing in Him even through the storms in our lives. Am I saying this is going to be easy? Absolutely not. But remember: with God, we can make it till the end as long as our faith is anchored in Him. Not by our own efforts — although this does not mean that we sit with our hands folded (unless God asks you to do just that) – but through the inner reliance we have in Him.

One lesson I have discovered in life is that this race is all about entering His rest and staying there. And our prayers need to be asking God to help us enter this place of rest He has created for us, regardless of the tumult around us.

 ***Journaling moment***

Now that you have read about Richard, Lola, Rachael and Jason, are there any lessons you can apply to your own situation? Are there changes you could make in your attitudes, beliefs and behaviours that could help you deal with your discouraged heart and troubled soul?

You might want to take a step back from your situation and reflect. Make notes in your journal and pray about what you uncover.

Don't let battle fatigue steal your joy

As we make our way through our life journeys, our battles can wear us out. We see a classic example of this in the life of Elijah who we have mentioned before. Despite our victories, exhaustion sets in and makes us act in ways we probably never expected. Over the years, I came to observe certain traits of my own, but hadn't taken time out to ponder them further – much less draw any parallel between how I was feeling and the great prophet's story. I had observed that, although God had brought me through great feats of my own, there were a few, but significant, occasions when I could not truly celebrate my triumphs. Whilst I did thank Father, it was not with the depth of worship I knew I could reach. During these times, it felt like I had become numb, as if I was stuck in limbo. This often made me feel guilty because I felt I ought to give God more but I just could not muster the energy to do so. I was worn out.

Then I noticed that, after a period of rest and a refreshing of my spirit, soul and body, I was back on form. My perspective changed, my focus realigned and I was ready for the world. And, as I began to look into this phenomenon, I realised that many of us experience battle fatigue to varying degrees – in the way a soldier might upon returning home from battle. However, if we don't manage our 'returning home' experience, as well as the fight preceding it, although the battle may have ended out there on the field, another battle is now being fought deep within us. We may come 'home' a war hero, with people around us celebrating the great things God has done in our lives, yet some of us sometimes struggle to see what the celebration is all about. Although we may be able to join in with those rejoicing with us to some extent, when we are left alone, our 'other' battle still rages on. On the outside we may look okay but, deep within us, we are wounded and bleeding.

When this happens, this inner war ends up sapping every last drop of our joy and depletes our energy. As with the life of Elijah, it affects the way we think, feel and act. In this state, we are open to negative emotions such as guilt, anger, fear, resentment and discouragement. Spiritually, we are weaker as we have most likely abandoned prayer, worship and reading of the Bible – the very things that strengthen, heal and uplift us. Physically, we may find ourselves prone to illnesses, especially those linked to stress and burnout. In short, this is not a good place to be.

Moving forward, there are three vital lessons I would like you to keep in mind:

1. Don't fight your own battles

Has your battle fatigue come about through trying to fight battles of your own, on your own? The Bible tells us that the battle is the Lord's – so maybe it is time to stop fighting and hand over the matter to God. (*Read 2 Chronicles 20.*) Handing over your battles does not mean taking a passive stance. Your weapon of war is your prayers. Fight your battles with this: your worship and the Word. Let God do the fighting for you. Stop trying to help Him out. He is quite capable. If you try to do so (and He has not asked it of you), you can end up creating an 'Ishmael' instead of an 'Isaac'. So stand and see the salvation of the Lord.

2. Don't underestimate the battle

More often than not, we don't know how long a particular journey, season or battle in our lives will be. We just know that we are in it. I think that we don't always give ourselves allowance for this. Instead, we try to carry on, business as usual, and then we wonder why we feel the way we do, during this difficult period and afterwards. Imagine having major heart surgery today and then deciding you are going into work tomorrow. Sounds absurd, right? But this is exactly what we do to ourselves in these situations and we end up putting undue stress on ourselves to get back in the race, pronto. We need to give ourselves a break and make the necessary allowances and changes in our lives. If, like Elijah, you have had your Mount Carmel experience then, trust me, you will need: 1) your 'wilderness' experience to recuperate; and 2) your 'Mount Sinai' time alone with God.

3. Don't walk alone

Getting God on board is especially essential during trying times, as we have seen. And, in addition to God-help, God also makes provision for us to receive support from others when needed. Having these two sources of support in place will help you pull through and recover more quickly. Over the years, I have come to value immensely the comfort God brings through people. It makes all the difference, not just in trying times but throughout ones life. Two, indeed, are better than one. When you are weak or when you fall, they are there to pull you up (*Ecclesiastes 4:9–12*).

In closing this section I just want to encourage you by emphasising the fact that, as children of God, it is indeed possible to come through a battle rejoicing and unscathed. Just ask Daniel who survived spending the night in a lion's den (*Daniel 6*). Ask Shadrach, Meshach, and Abed-Nego who not only survived a fiery furnace but did not even smell of smoke (*Daniel 3*). Ask Joseph whose dreams seemed to die when he was sold into slavery by his own brothers but who then became the prime minister of the nation that would save him and the rest of the children of Israel (*Genesis 37–50*). There are many more examples and I encourage you to explore the Bible for yourself and be encouraged but their testimonies. The same God that preserved them (mind, soul and body) can do the same for you.

Rather than being wearied or worried, comfort yourself with one of my favourite scriptures:

> '… Don't be afraid, I've redeemed you. I've called your name. You're mine.
> When you're in over your head, I'll be there with you.
> When you're in rough waters, you will not go down.
> When you're between a rock and a hard place, it won't be a dead end
> – Because I am God, your personal God, The Holy of Israel, your Saviour.
> I paid a huge price for you: all of Egypt, with rich Cush and Seba thrown in!
> That's how much you mean to me! That's how much I love you!

I'd sell off the whole world to get you back, trade the creation just for you.'
(*Isaiah 43:1–4, MSG*)

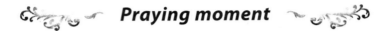 *Praying moment*

If you have experienced battle fatigue of your own, take a moment to say this prayer:

'Father, I recognise that the battles of life have worn me down. And as a result, I have not been myself. And so I invite you into this situation. Restore and heal me from my battles. Restore to me the joy of my salvation. Make me to hear joy and gladness and be satisfied. I ask for forgiveness for the times I may have wronged You through my attitudes and behaviours. I choose to be confident that though Heaven and Earth may pass away, Your love for me remains unyielding. And now I thank You because You always lead me to triumph, in Christ. For this, I worship You and give You my heartfelt praise.'

In Jesus' name. Amen.'

Chapter 8

Nuggets to strengthen your heart

> 'But those who wait for the Lord [who expect, look for, and hope in Him] shall change and renew their strength and power....'
> (*Isaiah 40:31, AMP*)

To help you on your journey, I have included some nuggets. As you read, I pray your heart becomes uplifted. May you experience true joy and be filled with strength as you make your way through this journey called life.

Keep the end in mind

> 'So if you're serious about living this new resurrection life with Christ, act like it. Pursue the things over which Christ presides. Don't shuffle along, eyes to the ground, absorbed with the things right in front of you. Look up, and be alert to what is going on around Christ – that's where the action is. See things from his perspective.'
> (*Colossians 3:1–2, MSG*)

The fact is, we are all here for a finite amount of time and our destination is Heaven. Hence, we need to ensure we keep things in perspective and keep our thoughts heavenward. Otherwise, we will get bogged down and entangled with life, losing hope and forgetting what waits ahead.

Paul had the right idea about this. Throughout his ministry, he was determined not only to run the race but to finish it and finish it well. If this is your intention as a believer, you might need to keep your eyes on your destination. See yourself as a voyager, travelling through this life and fulfilling the purpose God had for you, while you bring glory to Him and head back home. This may sound a tad morbid to you – but Heaven truly is our home. This world is only temporary.

Unless we start to see things this way, we stand a chance of losing the plot altogether –settling and laying down roots in the wilderness when we should be keeping the Promised Land in mind. At times, when I get discouraged about certain things, I have to ask myself whether the very thing I am stressing about will: 1) bring me closer to God; 2) help me fulfil my calling; or 3) keep me poised towards getting to Heaven.

When I use these criteria, I start to put things into

perspective. Then I realise that a number of the very things I am getting myself wound up about aren't actually helping me to achieve any of these criteria. They are simply desires of mine that could get in the way of my earthly assignment. Moreover, I find trends of our modern day life tend to filter in although God's Words say I am not to copy the behaviours and customs of the world (*Romans 12:2*). Yes, there are a hundred and one things I would like to have – but, when it comes to the bottom line, they would have no value in Heaven. They simply do not register on the heavenly scales.

So here is a suggestion: leave these modern-day behaviours and items in God's hands and endeavour not to get frazzled by not having them. One thing I am convinced of is that God will make provision for all our needs. Period. So let's just get on with Father's business, keeping our eyes on Jesus, expectant of the day He will return.

Monitor the seasons of your life

'A time to cry and a time to laugh.
A time to grieve and a time to dance.'
(*Ecclesiastes 3:4, NLT*)

We all go through different seasons in our life. And for each season, there is a time for everything. And so, if you feel stuck, ponder on whether you are taking the right action for the right season.

I remember when my father died, I had bottled up my feelings and did not open up to God —after all, He could have prevented it happening. I had tried to keep a brave face but, deep down inside, grief and anger ate away at me (the 'S.A.D. phase' described earlier). By not giving myself permission to grieve, I was stuck in limbo (the 'dormant phase') and could not move on with my life. I numbed myself with my work as it was something else to focus on (although I probably was not 'present' in the moment at all times).

When, a year or so after, I finally decided to share my feelings with God, I told Him how grieved I was at His taking my father away. And, lo and behold, the floodgates of my unshed tears were released and boy did I weep. I wept at the fact that I would never see my father again (on earth, that is). I wept that we had some 'unfinished business' we needed to resolve. I wept that my children would never get to know their grandfather. I wept that we would never take that trip to Asia we always said we would. And so, I wept in Gods presence and not once did He scold me, or tell me to 'get a grip' or 'be strong' (I hear the latter a lot).

He simply listened, and comforted me.

When the mourning period was up, when I felt Father say, 'It's time', He gave me the strength, supernaturally, to rise up. And, from that point on, I felt lighter. I felt myself lose my garments of mourning, layer by layer. In so doing, I became more hopeful. Though my earthly father had left me, my heavenly Father remained right by my side. And with the knowledge of my constant Companion, I was finally able to move past this episode in my life (the 'hopeful phase').

You, too, would do well to recognise the seasons of your life. Now would be a good time to reflect at your own life. Whilst your experience may not be the passing of a loved one, it may be that you have experienced loss of another kind – a dream, goal, marriage, good health, relationship, money, business, ministry perhaps. Maybe, now or in the past, you have experienced a challenging and/or perturbing situation. Have you really and truly moved on from it or are you stuck in the 'dormant phase'?

If so, maybe now is the time to bring it before God and lay it at the altar. Schedule some private time with Him and bring your thoughts, feelings and disappointments to Him. Trust me, He can handle it.

Stay in the race

'Therefore, since we are surrounded by such a huge crowd of witnesses to the life of faith, let us strip off every weight that slows us down, especially the sin that so easily trips us up. And let us run with endurance the race God has set before us.'
(*Hebrews 12:1, NLT*)

Whenever I read this scripture, I immediately picture myself running a race with crowds cheering me on. When my legs start to get tired and as I start to slow down, I look across and see some of my Biblical heroes cheering me on. I picture Paul telling me to not faint or get weary of doing good (*Galatians 6:9*). I can hear David telling me to encourage myself in the Lord (*I Samuel 30:6*). Nehemiah reminds me of the fact that the Joy of the Lord is my strength (*Nehemiah 8:10*). Esther encourages me with the fact that I was born for such a time as this (*Esther 4:14*). Joseph tells me that God will turn every evil plan to my good (*Genesis 50:20*). Elisha will shout across that things will be different this time tomorrow (*2 Kings 7:1*). The Shunammite woman will hold up a placard with 'It is well' written on it (*2 Kings 4*). When I look at the race ahead of me and feel I cannot run it, Jeremiah will remind me of the fact that nothing is impossible with God because nothing is too hard for Him (*Jeremiah*

32:17). And when I stumble and fall, Jesus will tell me to '*Talitha, cumi*,' which means, 'Little girl, I say to you, arise.' (*Mark 5:41*). With all this encouragement, I muster the strength to get to my feet and keep going.

And so, my heroes have become my personal cheerleading team – encouraging me along. They can be yours too. I take comfort knowing that others have gone before me and *walked in the same path* I now must take (life). That is why reading the scriptures is so important to keeping our joy, hope and strength. So I encourage you also to find heroes of your own. Read their stories and find out how they mustered strength to keep going even when it was against all odds. With such cheerleaders you will be encouraged every step of the way.

Maintain a thankful heart

> 'In everything give thanks …'
> (*1 Thessalonians 5:18, NKJ*)

Constantly remind yourself of the goodness of God. Thank Him for all that He has done, is doing and will do. You may not have everything you want today but He is still worthy. At times we get fixated on what is lacking in our lives and forget to thank God just because of who He is. As a result, we develop an ungrateful heart. Always remember that our appreciation and worship is not dependent on what God does or doesn't do. He deserves our thanks regardless of the outcome in our lives.

If you are struggling to find a reason to be thankful, take a trip down memory lane. Remind yourself of all the things God has done for you – large or small. Don't forget to thank Him for sending Jesus to die for your sins. The fact is, God has always been there for us all. Unlike us, He has been ever-faithful. His mercies are renewed daily towards us and that is the only reason we remain standing.

To help you with this, keep a regular journal of answered prayers, testimonies, miracles, blessings and breakthroughs. When you are feeling blue, pick up your journal and read it through. You will be amazed at all the great feats God had done – ones which you have lost sight of. I started doing this a few years ago and it always brings me to my knees when I recollect all that He has done. I believe David learnt this secret (as you will notice in the *Book of Psalms*) and, regardless of how tough his situation became, he always seemed to find the strength to worship God. I marvel that he could worship God straight after the death of the son Bathsheba bore him (*2 Samuel 12:20*). He was also the king who danced, unashamedly, before the Lord when the Ark of the Lord was returned to Jerusalem (*2 Samuel 6:14*). I believe this caught God's attention so that He promised that there would always be one of his descendants on the throne (*2 Samuel 7*). So, maybe you need to put on your dancing shoes and thank God ... just because ...

Learn to wait for God

> '... At the right time, I, the Lord, will make it happen.'
> (*Isaiah 60:22, NLT*)

If there is one lesson I have learned about God it is that He operates in times and seasons. This is reflected in our world – with night and day, winter and summer, birth and death, sowing and reaping, for example. He also operates these principles when it comes to dealing with us, our prayers, and our lives in general. He takes His time, puts plans into action and uses the concept of time to let them unfold in our lives. God is not confined to time as we know it, especially as the Bible mentions that a thousand years are as a passing day to God (*Psalm 90:4*).

We can be assured of the fact that our waiting is never

in vain. Despite what you might think, He is never too early or too late. He always shows up. Plus, He uses our waiting time to grow us and develop character in us – both of which can only be accomplished through time. So, regardless of what you may be facing today, rest assured that He is working on your behalf. And if He has given you a promise, be it spoken or written, He will bring it to pass. Resist the temptation to 'help' God or hurry things along. The outcome is never as good as God's original plan for us. So hold on, trust God and don't get discouraged. Delay is certainly not denial.

Maintain your dialogue with God

> 'Never stop praying.'
> (1 Thessalonians 5:17, NLT)

There is a tendency during trying or discouraging times to allow our precious time with God dwindle. This happens for many reasons such as our problems overwhelming us or even being disappointed with God. And when our issues become magnified in our eyes, it clouds our vision of the greatness of God. Before you know it, you no longer have a passion for Him or anything that will bring you closer to Him. In this state, you end up drifting away from God and make yourself open for the enemy to plant all manner of seeds in your heart (e.g. anger, fear and despair).

Therefore, you must do your utter best to maintain your communication with God, in whatever shape or form. Don't get caught up in religious 'dos and don'ts'. Find out what will work for you in the season you are in. I find that, when I really feel overwhelmed and exhausted by my challenges or life in general, I get into 'silent prayer' mode where I can pour out my heart to God for hours without opening my mouth. I may lie in bed, on the floor, or even talk to Him as I am driving. Other modes I adopt are: writing down my prayers and finding scriptures or songs that help me communicate my thoughts, feelings and prayers to God. In turn, I receive His comfort and strength to keep going.

In the Bible, David opted to write Psalms to God. Paul and Silas worshipped God at midnight (*Acts 16*). Jesus Christ, whilst in agony, prayed earnestly till His sweat became like great drops of blood (*Luke 22:40–44*). It does not matter what format you use, as long as you keep your heart engaged with Him. And if find you have drifted away or are struggling with this, get the support of others to help you get back on track (e.g. prayer partners and accountability partners). Lastly, always remember that God is closer than you think.

Guard your heart! Resist discouraging thoughts

'The thief's purpose is to steal and kill and destroy. My purpose is to give them a rich and satisfying life.'
(*John 10:10, NLT*)

Have you noticed that one minute you can be fine and the next you feel down for no apparent reason? The chances are a thought drifted into your mind and you pondered on it. Then, before you knew it, it had taken root and, lo and behold, you feel down in the dumps. I believe this is an attack of the enemy and we need to be mindful of it.

The Bible tells us that the thief (i.e. the devil) comes to steal, kill and destroy (*John 10:10*) and I believe this is one of his strategies to steal our joy. If we do not identify and resist such thoughts, we will find ourselves on a downward spiral towards discouragement – one which we may find it difficult to pull ourselves out of. So it is essential to nip such thoughts in the bud. To do this, simply say a quick prayer and use God's Word to act as a shield to what is infecting your mind. Your prayer could go like this:

'I come against the spirit of discouragement in Jesus' Name. I take authority of any strongholds of the

mind. The Joy of the Lord is my strength.
My mind has been renewed and I have the mind of Christ.
No weapon formed or fashioned against me will prosper, in Jesus' name.'

If you are struggling with such thoughts, call someone and ask them to pray for you and with you. Don't let the enemy gain a foothold in your mind by sowing seeds of discouragement (or others) in your mind. Because the seeds he sows today become forests tomorrow.

Stop trying to figure God out

'You will guard him and keep him in perfect and constant peace whose mind [both its inclination and its character] is stayed on You, because he commits himself to You, leans on You, and hopes confidently in You.'
(*Isaiah 26:3, NKJ*)

When going through trying times, I find my efforts to rationalise the situation often prove to be futile. Before I cottoned on that I simply needed to trust God, I would look under every stone, questioning myself and wondering what I had or hadn't done, and trying to figure out why God had not come through.

It drove me nuts! I realised that if I wanted to remain on this side of sanity, I needed to fix my mind on God and leave the matter in His hands.

However, I noticed this not only happened in trying times but also when I worried where my life was heading. I couldn't help but wonder what the future held. I wanted to know what God was up to so I could 'plan' around it. However, after many years of frustration, I finally came to the end of myself. I had pulled my hair out long enough so I simply decided that I could no longer live this way – disguising my anxiety, doubt and fear. So I gave myself the permission to break from this way of living and quit trying to figure God out. Stumbling upon *Isaiah 26:3*, I realised I needed to lean confidently on Him, trusting He would come through for me and that He had a good plan for me. And when I embraced this, I started to experience real peace.

I believe when we get to the place of relinquishing everything to God in faith, that is when we will start to experience the fullness of His joy. God has a plan for you and it will surely come to pass. So combat your need to figure things out by yourself.

When in doubt, ask!

> 'Call to me and I will answer you. I'll tell you marvellous and wondrous things that you could never figure out on your own.'
> (*Jeremiah 33:3, MSG*)

A quality I admire in David is his constant desire to seek what God's thoughts were on a matter. He sought God before taking action. One particular example of this that stood out for me was when he enquired of the Lord whether to attack the Philistines who were attacking the city of Keilah (*1 Samuel 23:1–5*). God said 'yes' and David went to tell his men God's response. But they were afraid and did not want to go. So David went back to God to confirm what He had said. Gods answer was still the same and this gave David the confidence to persuade his men and lead them to victory.

I mention this simply because there are times when we may get doubtful, lose our way or our present circumstances seem to be conflicting with what God has said to us. You may be holding onto a word or a promise from God which you were so sure of but, as time passed, you had begun to wonder. In such times, the solution is simply to go back to God and find out His view on the matter. By doing this, we gain the strength to march on ahead, despite what we see.

A stumbling block that can get in our way of our doing this is the idea some of us have that God does not talk to us anymore. This gives us the impression that He is far removed from us. All totally and utterly untrue. God is concerned about every detail of our lives and it is His absolute delight and pleasure when we approach Him. It is the very thing He wants us to do. So He should be the very first Person we go to. According to *Jeremiah 33:3*, He invites us to seek Him and He may choose to respond in a plethora of ways. Moreover, you don't need to be a prophet to hear God's voice! Seek Him conscientiously enough and He shall be found.

I know for sure that when we pursue Him with all our heart, He will speak. He will lead us, guiding us into all truths. Our challenge is: 1) believing that He indeed speaks and expecting Him to do so; 2) committing to the act of pursuit – a demonstration of our desires; 3) getting rid of preconceived ideas and expectations; 4) developing a listening ear and receptive heart; 5) getting rid of all the background 'noises' in our lives so we can hear the still, small voice of God speaking to us; 6) being still and remaining long enough in His presence.

Get past all of these and you position yourself to hear. So the next time you are in prayer, say to God, 'Speak Lord for your servant is listening' as young Samuel did (*1 Samuel 3:10*).

Ask for help

'Two people are better off than one, for they can help each other succeed. If one person falls, the other can reach out and help. But someone who falls alone is in real trouble.' (*Ecclesiastes 4:10–11, NLT*)

Thankfully, God has made provision of help, for all of us, in our times of need. Help comes in all shapes and sizes but the most important thing to do is ask for it. Don't let pride or anything else rob you of the support you need, irrespective of who you are or what you have accomplished. Examples of the types of help to ask for include:

- prayer – you can ask one or more people to pray for and with you

- encouragement – through an encouraging word, sharing of scripture, inspiring literature, etc.

- counselling, advice and guidance

- accountability – you can make yourself accountable to others for various reasons such as to combat negative thoughts, get into a routine of reading of the Bible or praying

- staying with people – depending on your situation and feasibility, you could decide to spend time in the home of people such as friends or family

In terms of whom to ask, look around you. Who has God placed around you? Do you have one or more trusted friends, family, church members, someone in your church leadership team, a support group or network, etc. who you can ask? If the answer is 'no', I encourage you to prayerfully find someone whom you can enlist for help. We should all have someone in our lives that we can seek for help. The reality is, we cannot make it alone and God never designed it to be so. Jesus enlisted the help of His disciples to fulfil His mission. And just before His arrest in the Garden of Gethsemane, He called upon His closest three to support Him in prayer. This, too, has to be the model we adopt in our lives, regardless of your perception of your faith, maturity, status, etc.

The good news is that God has already positioned people in our lives to help us on many levels – physically, spiritually, and emotionally. Moreover, it is not just about us receiving, but also about reciprocating in the lives of others who might need help too.

Create an uplifting living environment

> '...In Your presence, there is fullness of Joy ...'
> (*Psalm 16:11, NKJ*)

This is all about creating an atmosphere in your living space and workspace (if possible) that uplifts you. First and foremost, fill your space with God. Invite Him into your home (and workplace). Pray against the spirit of discouragement and depression that may have taken up residence there. Command it to leave in the name of Jesus. Take charge of the atmosphere by speaking into existence what you want the atmosphere of your home to be like – e.g. joyful, peaceful, stress free, restful, calming, healing, etc. Regularly anoint your home with oil. This can be aided with scripture or godly music playing in the background. I often pray over my bed as the night season tends to be when anxiety and unrest come about. I also anoint my bed.

Secondly, fill your space with life (e.g. people, plants,

pets), uplifting music, inspiring words (e.g. books, teaching, affirmations), vibrant pictures and colours, aromas and anything that you feel will give you a lift. I like to have soothing music playing in the background day and night. When cooking, I can listen to one of my favourite preachers or teachers. I have scriptures I regularly use to confess over my life and so on. I do this because I want to create the right environment in my home, one that is uplifting. If I were to be passive about this, I could easily find myself allowing any old nonsense to fill my head, and ultimately my heart. And if I listen to certain TV and radio stations, by the end of the day it will be all doom and gloom. So I have to be proactive about this, in addition to the daily routines of prayer, Bible reading, and so on.

Therefore, I encourage you to create the right atmosphere around you, especially in your living space. Now there may not be much you can do when you step out of your home but at least you can fortify yourself as much as you can. Watch out whom you allow to speak into your life. Be mindful of the books you read and to what you watch and listen. At some point, they will germinate and bear fruit if you let them. Like weeds, they will take over.

Chapter 9
Uplifting Scriptures

God's love for you

'For his unfailing love toward those who fear him is as great as the height of the heavens above the earth.'
(*Psalm 103:11, NLT*)

'If you then, being evil, know how to give good gift to your children, how much more will you Father who is in heaven give good gifts to those who ask Him.'
(*Matthew 7: 11, NKJ*)

'He who did not spare His own Son, but delivered Him up for us all, how shall He not with Him also freely give us all things?'
 (*Romans 8:32, NKJ*)

'Observe how Christ loved us. His love was not cautious but extravagant. He didn't love in order to get something from us but to give everything of himself to us…'
(*Ephesians. 5:2, MSG*)

'… casting all your care upon Him for He cares for you.'
(*1 Peter 5:7, NKJ*)

God's will for your life

'With long life I will satisfy him, And show him My salvation.'
(*Psalm 91:16, NKJ*)

'I shall not die, but live, and declare the works of the LORD.'
(*Psalm 118:17, NKJ*)

'Yet God has made everything beautiful for its own time…'
(*Ecclesiastes 3:11, NLT*)

'I know what I'm doing. I have it all planned out – plans to take care of you, not abandon you, plans to give you the future you hope for.'
(*Jeremiah 29:11, MSG*)

'The thief does not come except to steal, and to kill, and to destroy. I have come that they may have life, and that they may have it more abundantly.'
(*John 10:10, NKJ*)

God's word concerning your wellbeing

'...For I am the Lord who heals you.'
(*Exodus 15:26, NLT*)

'HE LORD is my Shepherd [to feed, guide, and shield me], I shall not lack. He makes me lie down in [fresh, tender] green pastures; He leads me beside the still and restful waters. He refreshes and restores my life (my self)....'
(*Psalm 23:1-3, AMP*)

'If your heart is broken, you'll find God right there; if you're kicked in the gut, he'll help you catch your breath.'
(*Psalm 34.18, MSG*)

'The Lord nurses them when they are sick and restores them to health.'
(*Psalm 41:3, NLT*)

'He gives power to the weak and strength to the powerless. Even youths will become weak and tired, and young men will fall in exhaustion. But those who trust in the Lord will find new strength. They will soar high on wings like eagles. They will run and not grow weary. They will walk and not faint.'
(*Isaiah 40:29–31, NLT*)

'But He was wounded for our transgressions, He was bruised for our iniquities; The chastisement for our peace was upon Him, And by His stripes we are healed.'
(Isaiah 53:5, NKJ)

'For I will restore health to you and heal you of your wounds," says the LORD…'
(Jeremiah 30:17, NKJ)

'I'll refresh tired bodies; I'll restore tired souls.'
(Jeremiah 31:25, MSG)

'But for your who fear my name, the Sun of Righteousness will rise with healing in his wings. And you will go free, leaping with joy like calves let out to pasture.'
(Malachi 4:2, NLT)

'But if the Spirit of Him who raised Jesus from the dead dwells in you, He who raised Christ from the dead will also give life to your mortal bodies through His Spirit who dwells in you.' *(Rom 8:11, NKJ)*

God always comes through

'…be strong and courageous! Do not be afraid or

discouraged. For the Lord your God is with you wherever you go.'
(*Joshua 1:9, NLT*)

'For I know that my Redeemer and Vindicator lives, and at last He [the Last One] will stand upon the earth.'
(*Job 19:25, AMP*)

'Let be and be still, and know (recognize and understand) that I am God. I will be exalted among the nations! I will be exalted in the earth!'
(*Psalm 46:10, AMP*)

'My heart is confident in you, O God; my heart is confident. No wonder I can sing your praises!'
(*Psalm 57:7, NLT*)

'Tell the godly that all will be well for them....'
(*Isaiah 3:10, NLT*)

'"Do not weep any longer, for I will reward you", says the Lord.'
(*Jeremiah 31:16, NLT*)

'"Do not be afraid; only believe."'
(*Mark 5:36, NKJ*)

'DO NOT let your hearts be troubled [distressed, agitated]. You believe in and adhere to and trust in and rely on God; believe in and adhere to and trust in and rely also on Me.'
(*John 14:1, AMP*)

'...He himself gives life and breath to everything, and he satisfies every need.'
(*Acts 17:25, NLT*)

'Don't fret or worry. Instead of worrying, pray. Let petitions and praises shape your worries into prayers, letting God know your concerns. Before you know it, a sense of God's wholeness, everything coming together for good, will come and settle you down. It's wonderful what happens when Christ displaces worry at the centre of your life.'
(*Philippians 4:6–7, MSG*)

'And let the peace [soul harmony which comes] from Christ rule [act as umpire continually] in your hearts [deciding and settling with finality all questions that arise in your minds, in that peaceful state] to which as [members of Christ's] one body you were also called [to live]. And be thankful [appreciative], [giving praise to God always].
(*Colossians 3:15, AMP*)

'So take a new grip with your tired hands and strengthen your weak knees. Mark out a straight path for your feet so that those who are weak and lame will not fall but become strong.'
(*Hebrews 12:12–13, NLT*)

God is with you

'...I will not leave you nor forsake you.'
(*Joshua 1:5, NKJ*)

'For by You I can run against a troop, By my God I can leap over a wall.'
(*Psalm 18:29, NKJ*)

'The Lord is my light and my salvation – so why should I be afraid? The Lord is my fortress, protecting me from danger, so why should I tremble?'
(*Psalm 27:1, NLT*)

'God is our refuge and strength, always ready to help in times of trouble. So we will not fear when earthquakes come and the mountains crumble into the sea.'
(*Psalm 46:1–2, NLT*)

'God is in the midst of her, she shall not be moved; God shall help her, just at the break of dawn.'
(*Psalm 46:5, NKJ*)

'From the end of the earth will I cry to You, when my heart is overwhelmed and fainting; lead me to the rock that is higher than I [yes, a rock that is too high for me].'
(*Psalm 61:2, AMP*)

'I will be your God throughout your lifetime – until your hair is white with age. I made you, and I will care for you. I will carry you along and save you.'
(*Isaiah 46:4, NLT*)

'… Yet I am not alone because the Father is with me.'
(*John 16:32, NLT*)

'He comes alongside us when we go through hard times, and before you know it, he brings us alongside someone else who is going through hard times so that we can be there for that person just as God was there for us.'
(*2 Corinthians 1:3–4, MSG*)

'… "My grace is sufficient for you, for my power is made perfect weakness."'
(*2 Corinthians 12:9, NKJ*)

'For I can do all things through Christ who gives me strength.'
(*Philippians 4:13, NLT*)

'And this same God who takes care of me will supply all your needs from his glorious riches, which have been given to us in Christ Jesus.'
(*Philippians 4:19, NLT*)

God is able

'God is not a man, that He should lie, nor a Son of man that He should repent. Has He said, and will He not do? Or has He spoken, and will He not make it good?'
(*Numbers 23:19, NKJ*)

'Dear God, my Master, you created earth and sky by your great power – by merely stretching out your arm! There is nothing you can't do.'
(*Jeremiah 32:17, MSG*)

'..."With men this is impossible, but with God all things are possible."'
(*Matthew 19:26, NKJ*)

'For nothing is impossible with God.'
(*Luke 1:37, NKJ*)

'... Even if everyone else is a liar, God is true. ...'
(*Romans 3:4, NLT*)

'So God has given both his promise and his oath. These two things are unchangeable because it is impossible for God to lie. Therefore, we who have fled to him for refuge can have great confidence as we hold to the hope that lies before us.'
(*Hebrews 6:18, NLT*)

'Jesus Christ is the same yesterday, today, and forever.'
(*Hebrews 13:8, NKJ*)

Afterword

'Stand up, pick up your mat, and walk.'
(*Mark 2:9, NLT*)

As we draw to an end, you may wonder what gives me the audacity to share this book with you. Well, like you, 'life happened' to me too. The book came about through seeking answers to questions of my own that surfaced when I faced challenges. So I see the book as presenting you with lessons (and, at times, hard facts) that I felt God was sharing with me.

As it might be in your case, there were times I did not want to hear what God was saying because I could not look past what I felt was God's to-do list (my prayers, questions, etc.). It seemed that He was sitting on it and doing nothing. And so, this made writing some sections of this book a painful journey for me. Tears often streamed down my face as I came face-to-face with some harsh truths God was teaching me. I too, you see, had to *swallow the same pills* I have prescribed in this book. And I say that because I don't want you to feel like you are the only one to feel the way you do or that someone is preaching something they have not lived. Trust me – been there, bought the T-shirt and written the book!

One thing I am certain about is that God does not want us to remain in a state of discouragement. That is not His personal best for us nor does it reflect the abundant life He planned for us. And so, it is my sincere belief that God can and will make your heart smile again. The smile I refer to includes an internal joy and the confidence that all will be well. The question is, whether you are willing to confront all that has brought you to this place (e.g. disappointment, challenging experiences, and other contributory factors). I use the word 'willing' because it is a conscious choice you need to make.

I want to leave you with some parting thoughts wherever you may find yourself today on the continuum of discouragement and complete joy. Use them as reminders on your journey in life.

God is with you

> '...If God is for us, who can be against us?'
> (*Romans 8:31, NKJ*)

One theme I am hoping you have picked up from this book is the fact that God is mindful of His own. He loves you dearly and will come through for you.

All will be well

'And we know that God causes everything to work together for the good of those who love God and are called according to his purpose for them.'
(*Romans 8:28, NLT*)

Despite what you might be going through (and coming out of, for sure), be rest-assured that everything will be okay. Things will work out, you just wait and see. One day, you will look back and marvel at the goodness of God in your life.

In closing

I encourage you to keep God at the centre of your life. I have discovered that this is the sure tonic to cure a discouraged heart and troubled soul. Keep your eyes fixed solely on Him rather than the problem. Pray to God in faith, obey His Word and leave the consequences to Him.

Lastly, always carry in your heart the fact that He loves you. You are the apple of His eyes. You are special to Him.

Praying moments

'I pray that God Almighty touches the recesses of your heart so you can experience complete joy for the remainder of your days. May He give you the strength so you can keep going, no matter what. May your hopes in God never be deferred. And may your heart smile again, in Jesus' name. Amen'

'MY HEART MAY FAIL, AND MY SPIRIT MAY GROW WEAK, BUT GOD REMAINS THE STRENGTH OF MY HEART; HE IS MINE FOREVER.'

(PSALM 73:26, NLT)

About the author

Gladys Famoriyo is an award-winning author, inspirational speaker, consultant and professional coach with many years of international experience. She is the author of the book, *Overcoming Emotional Baggage: a Woman's Guide to Living the Abundant Life* that promotes emotional wellbeing and restoration, based on Biblical principles. Gladys is the Founder/Host of various emotional wellbeing and restorative initiatives, programmes and conferences including the *Overcoming Emotional Baggage Women's Conference*. Alongside these, she has published of a number of emotional wellbeing resources, applicable for individual use as well as within a small group setting.

Gladys is the Founder/Director of Success Partners Limited, an award-winning consulting and training leader for the development and wellbeing of women. Success Partners Ltd runs the Gladys Famoriyo Academy which trains, mentors and coaches authors, speakers, leaders, business owners, entrepreneurs and coaches.

Gladys is also the Founder of Gladys Famoriyo Ministries which teaches practical principles to promote spiritual growth and emotional restoration through books, resources, conferences and the media.

Gladys speaks to audiences worldwide and is best known for her 'can-do' approach as well as her ability to inspire and challenge her audiences to action. As a published writer, Gladys has written numerous published articles for several international publications. Currently, she is a regular columnist for *The Christian Post* (USA) and *Keep The Faith* (UK) where she continues to use her writing as a medium to influence people positively, worldwide. Gladys has also appeared on many international TV and radio stations such as the BBC and Premier Christian Radio and has also been featured in international magazines.

Find out more about Gladys Famoriyo, along with her services, products and upcoming events, at www.gladysf.com.

Follow Gladys Famoriyo on Facebook, Twitter, and Linkedin. Read her blogs and sign up for her free inspiring eNewsletter at www.gladysf.com

Contact her UK office at:

Gladys Famoriyo
Newmarket 4,
Keys Business Village,
Keys Park Road,
Hednesford, Staffordshire,
United Kingdom
WS12 2HA

Tel: +44 (0) 870 750 1969 Email: info@gladysf.com

Also available from the author

Milestones International Publishers
ISBN 0-924748-73-7

To order, call +44 (0) 870 750 1969 or email
orders@gladysfbooks.com

Visit us online at www.gladysfbooks.com

Also available at book retailers

It's Time To Ditch The Baggage!

On our journeys in life, we experience challenges and/or perturbing situations that may result in hurt, pain, disappointment, grief and separation, leaving many of us emotionally battered, bruised and wounded. As a result, many end up accumulating emotional baggage.

Often, our busy and cluttered lives mean we have little or no time to deal with this as there are goals, tasks and busy schedules that must be kept up with.

Hence, we tend to bury our heads in the sand, get back on our treadmills and try our best to get on with life - with our unresolved or unfinished issues in tow. To hide our issues or deal with our inner unrest, we adopt techniques such as wearing masks, comfort eating and retail therapy, though they don't serve us.

Therefore, Overcoming Emotional Baggage is the perfect book for women who want to live their lives baggage free. Based on biblical principles, this book will support you in uncovering your baggage and empower you to start your journey to wholeness. Filled with useful exercises and practical insights, this book is a valuable resource for individual use as well as in a small group setting.

I am amazed and delighted. Powerful and much needed information.
- Dr. Wanda A. Davis-Turner - Speaker & Author. USA

If you have faced disappointments, you will receive strength and support from reading this book. Those involved in ministering to and mentoring women will also find this a useful reference.
- Millicent Brown – Director, Women's Ministries
New Testament Church of God. UK

Powerful, analytical and definitely life-changing! More than just another self-help book. Soothes the soul, revives the spirit and restores the mind.
- Sharon Platt McDonald - Director, Health Ministries
British Union Conference of Seventh-day Adventists.
Author, Healing Hearts; Restoring Minds. UK

Also available from GF Books LTD

Overcoming Emotional Baggage for Women Self-Study Coaching Programme by Gladys Famoriyo

ISBN 978-0-9562606-1-1

This comprehensive, self-paced coaching programme takes you through the essence of the book, *Overcoming Emotional Baggage: A Woman's Guide to Living the Abundant Life* (Gladys Famoriyo). Designed with you in mind, the *Overcoming Emotional Baggage for Women* programme contains powerful insights, principles, questions and activities that aim to empower you to take positive action to move you forward in your personal emotional development.

Our step-by-step, supportive programme acts as your own personal coach, guiding you through your journey to optimum emotional wellbeing. The *Overcoming Emotional Baggage for Women* programme is an excellent companion for the book, *Overcoming Emotional Baggage: A Woman's Guide to Living the Abundant Life*, and a must-have resource for women intent on living effective lives, as it helps you put what you have read into the necessary practice.

Overcoming Emotional Baggage for Small Groups by Gladys Famoriyo

ISBN 978-0-9562606-1-1

This comprehensive guide provides facilitators with guidelines on how to run powerful group sessions using the book, *Overcoming Emotional Baggage: A Woman's Guide To Living The Abundant Life* (Gladys Famoriyo).

This handy resource tells facilitators exactly what to do AND say – meaning preparation time is kept to a minimum. The session planner also provides information, tips and tools on how to effectively run a life-changing group. Simple to use, the planner is an invaluable resource for both experienced and novice facilitators.

eWoman Group Facilitator Toolkit: Running an Effective Group by Gladys Famoriyo

ISBN: 978-0-9562606-0-4

This practical toolkit provides you with everything you need to know about starting and running an effective eWoman Group. The toolkit simplifies the task of starting a group and is packed full of information, techniques, strategies and tips to help you run a successful group. Comprehensive, yet simple to use, the toolkit is an invaluable resource for serious facilitators.

To order, call +44 (0) 870 750 1969 (UK) or email orders@gladysfbooks.com
Visit us online at www.gladysfbooks.com

Initiatives from the author

Introducing eWoman Groups - empowering, enlightening and encouraging women

Meet ~ Share ~ Learn

eWoman Groups is all about promoting the wellbeing and development of women. It is the place where you meet other women, share experiences, and learn strategies to promote your own wellbeing.

Each eWoman Group, led by a facilitator, work through the *Overcoming Emotional Baggage for Women* programme based on the inspiring, coaching book, *Overcoming Emotional Baggage: A Woman's Guide To Living The Abundant Life*. In this supportive forum, women can learn powerful insights and practical tips to promote and maintain their emotional wellbeing. Through the use of peer support and insightful discussions, women will feel empowered to take positive action and move forward with their lives.

In short, eWoman Groups is all about women helping themselves in the company of other like-minded women. eWoman Groups can be used within established groups and organisations or can be set up as a stand alone group.

To find out more about eWoman Groups including future facilitator training programmes or to download a free guide, log on to www.gladysf.com.

To order your eWoman Group resources, call +44 (0) 870 750 1969
or email orders@gladysfbooks.com.
Visit us online at www.gladysfbooks.com

My Journal

My Journal

My Journal

My Journal

My Journal

My Journal

My Journal

My Journal

GF BOOKS

GF Books LTD

Changing lives through words

www.gladysfbooks.com